Above and Beyond

*The incredible story of Frank Luke Jr.
Arizona's Medal of Honor
Flying Ace of the First World War.*

Keith Warren Lloyd

All Rights Reserved. Copyright © 2015 by Keith Warren Lloyd

*"They were still so young they hadn't learned
to count the odds and to sense they might
owe the universe a tragedy."*

Norman Maclean
Young Men and Fire

Chapter One

Verdun is a clean and orderly village astride the banks of the River Meuse in a quiet, rural section of eastern France. It is a short journey from the village center, on a road that winds through wooded countryside, to a great cathedral that stands on the crest of a hill. The sight is at once breathtakingly beautiful and hauntingly silent, a memorial to the many thousands who gave their lives.

It is here in soldierly rows beneath a carpet of lush grass that they are interned, on the same hallowed ground where they fought so desperately to save their beloved France. It is here that they fulfilled their solemn pledge to one another: *On Ne Passé Pas*. They shall not pass.

Beyond the stone crosses of the fallen lie more emerald fields and scattered woods of broadleaf trees. Even today the rolling meadows bear scars from the Great War. The grass grows rich and green within subtle undulations that were once trenches.

It was in these trenches that the blue-coated French *poilus* and khaki-clad British *tommies* faced the grey legions of invading Germans across a few yards of treacherous no-man's-land. Later the weary allied armies were joined by fresh American troops, who at first seemed brash and confident but would soon be indoctrinated to the harsh realities of total war.

In these same trenches the infantrymen of 1914-1918 became acquainted with the misery of mud, rats, dysentery, rotten food and immersion foot. Along with discomfort came death; it was abundant and its horror had arrived in many new forms. There were seemingly endless barrages of artillery shells, chattering machine guns, rumbling steel tanks and yellow clouds of poisonous gas. Scores of men would die to gain a few scant yards, cut down by automatic fire as they struggled through shell holes and barbed wire entanglements, only to lose the same ground to the enemy the next day.

Soaring high above it all was yet another new weapon: the airplane.

*   *   *   *

Although enviable by front-line infantry standards, the dugout where Jerry Vasconcelles found himself in September of 1918 was far from safe and comfortable. As a Captain in the Air Service branch of the United States Army Signal Corps, he commanded the advanced airfield of the 27th Aero Squadron, placed close to the front near Verdun and well within range of the heavy German guns. The airstrip served as a re-fueling and re-arming point for the airplanes of the First Pursuit Group, the pilots of which had been working hard all month to support the American offensive drive in the Saint Mihiel sector.

On this particular day, Jerry peered skyward from the dugout that served as his command post. It was late afternoon and the sky was beginning to darken. The artillery of both sides rumbled in the distance. As expected, there soon came the humming of an aircraft motor, and a stubby Spad pursuit plane drifted gracefully downward to land among the backfilled shellholes.

Jerry crossed the field to where the Spad had rolled to a stop, dreading the task that he had to perform. A few minutes earlier he had received a telephone call from the commander of the 27th Aero Squadron, Captain Alfred A. Grant. Jerry had been ordered to place the Spad pilot, one Second Lieutenant Frank Luke Junior, under arrest.

The tough, incorrigible kid from Arizona had really gotten himself into trouble this time, Jerry mused. After a scathing reprimand from Captain Grant, Luke had taken off from the 27th squadron's main airfield at Rembercourt within minutes of being grounded by his commanding officer. Luke had only been in France a short while, but had already developed a reputation for being hard-headed and boastful, with a disdain for authority and the annoying habit of wandering off whenever the mood struck him.

Over the past month, however, Luke had destroyed four German airplanes and ten of their heavily-protected observation balloons, making him the reigning American "ace-of-aces," the fighter pilot with the most air-to-air victories. But his amazing run of death-defying feats was coming to an end. Luke would be shipped back to headquarters under guard and would surely be court-martialed.

The young man that emerged from the cockpit of the biplane possessed the lean, muscular body of an athlete. With his close-cropped blond hair and hawk-like features, he looked very much like the German youngsters that he fought against. The blue eyes held a vacant, faraway look, for the twenty-one year old had recently lost a close friend, and had been involved in a great deal of violence in the past weeks.

Vasconcelles was spared the unpleasant task of arresting Luke. From the sky above came the droning of another airplane engine. The next incoming fighter was a Sopwith Camel flown by Major Harold Hartney, the commanding officer of the First Pursuit Group, the parent command of the 27th Aero Squadron. Hartney knew of the row between Grant and Luke and decided to fly up to the advanced field to settle the matter.

Hartney had shown remarkable patience with Luke since his arrival in France and had recognized the potential of this incredibly brave, if obstinate, young man. After landing, Hartney listened to Luke's request to attack three German observation balloons that were moored along the River Meuse near the village of Avecourt. The veteran commander relented, as long as Luke agreed to wait until sundown.

Just before six o'clock, the 235-horsepower Hisso engine lifted Luke's Spad from the grassy field and into the growing darkness…

*   *   *   *

In order to understand Frank Luke, one must first understand Arizona.

Theodore Roosevelt Junior understood it. Willing or not, as the son of the soldier, statesman, and daredevil with an unquenchable zest for life, Teddy Junior was taken along on many of his father's adventures. It was then that he became familiar with the kind of men who tamed the southwestern frontier.

In an essay he penned about Frank Luke, who served in the same 1st Pursuit Group as his brother Quentin, Roosevelt wrote of "barren, sun-scorched deserts, the desolate wind-weathered mountains and buttes," and about the "cattlemen, sheep men, prospectors; and with them the gunfighters, gamblers and bad men that go with the frontier. They were restless, adventurous young men of the nation."

It was into this world that Frank Luke Junior was born on 19 May 1897, a full fifteen years before Arizona achieved statehood. At the time Phoenix was a small but thriving farming community of 5500 souls in the Salt River Valley. It took a hard person to live and work in Phoenix in those times; one had to contend with everything from scorching desert heat and diamondback rattlesnakes to monsoon storms and rock-hard *coliche* soil.

Frank Luke Senior had arrived in Phoenix in 1873. A German immigrant, he had served in the Union Army before becoming a miner and later a shopkeeper. Frank married a girl of French and German descent, Otilia "Tillie" Libenow, and together they settled into a home on East Washington Street in Phoenix. Frank Junior was the fifth of their nine children.

The children of Arizona often grow up as rugged as the land they live in. Skin is burned dark by the sun, bare feet are thickened by days of running and playing on the parched, thorny ground of washes and jagged foothills. Frank soon proved to be an independent and energetic youngster, always ready to embark upon some sort of adventure.

"Frank was always a good boy," his mother said of him, "but ever since he had been big enough to toddle, he had been into everything, for he was full of life."

Quickly developing a restless spirit, Frank was happiest when he was outdoors. By the age of twelve it was becoming difficult to keep him at home. Often accompanied by his two close friends, Albert Pinney and Bill Elder, Frank would roam the Arizona back country on hunting and fishing trips. A good horse and a good rifle were standard equipment, and like many Arizona boys in the early twentieth century, Frank became a crack shot. Together the boys roamed for incredible distances, as far north as the White Mountains, nearly 200 miles north of Phoenix, and as far south as the border with Mexico. One of their favorite spots for exploration was the Superstition Mountain range, thirty miles east of Phoenix, as treacherous and rugged a territory as Arizona has to offer. Many gold prospectors and explorers found it easy to get lost in the Superstitions, where each sun-baked, rocky trail led to a hopelessly dry, cactus-studded ravine that looked identical to the last.

One of Frank's most notorious misadventures happened during one of these trips to the back country. South of the notorious cavalry outpost of Fort Apache, Frank and Bill Elder rode their horses across many miles of rough trails that cut through desert plateau dotted with gnarled juniper trees, their horses leaving clouds of powdery dust in their wake. At the bottom of a canyon the two boys encountered White River, a normally fast-moving stream fed by the melting snow of the Mogollon Rim, but this day it had been swollen to a rushing torrent by a recent monsoon. The Apaches warned the boys against crossing and advised them to turn back. Frank, displaying the stubborn nature that was fast becoming a trademark, started to ford the rising river against their advice.

The decision cost the boys their unfortunate pack mule, the braying creature swept downstream by the relentless current along with most of their supplies. The diminutive Bill Elder was also swept off his horse by the raging water and seemed likely to suffer the same fate. Acting swiftly, Frank dove into the river and swam to Bill's rescue, grabbing the smaller boy by the hair and dragging him to a nearby eddy to save his life.

The White River tale serves as an early glimpse into the psyche of Frank Luke; like many of the young, rough-hewn outdoorsmen found in the American Southwest, he could be adventuresome and daring but also hard-headed and impatient. At the same time Frank was capable of selfless courage, willing to put himself in harm's way to protect a friend without a thought of his own safety.

Frank's penchant for mischief and adventure followed him onto the grounds Phoenix Union High School. He found his niche as a member of the football team, where cultivated physical toughness added to his reputation.

"He was the nerviest and coolest-headed football player I ever saw," Coach Francis Geary said of Frank.

An aggressive tailback, Luke once fractured a collar bone during a playoff game but refused to be benched. By his senior year, Luke was a lean, strong 5 feet 10 inches and 155 pounds.

Luke also lettered in baseball and track, played basketball and tennis and was on the boxing squad.

Another glimpse into the mind of this restless young man comes from an incident that must have scared the faculty at Phoenix Union to death. Either for laughs or out of pure reckless curiosity, Luke fashioned a homemade parachute from a large umbrella and planned to jump from the roof a three- story school building. A large crowd gathered on the grass below, apparently to watch their slightly-crazed football captain plummet to his end. The principal, alerted by the growing number of spectators, went outside to investigate and talked Frank out of the stunt. Luke had to be content with watching a makeshift dummy drop to the ground in his place.

After high school Frank gained employment at the New Cornelia Copper Company in Ajo, Arizona, in the arid desert hills just north of the border with Mexico.

Luke was hired to help with a newly-patented copper processing procedure, where huge chunks of copper ore from the nearby mine were crushed to pieces and fed by conveyor belt into concrete tanks fitted with anodes and cathodes. The ore was then bathed in acid and refined by electrolysis. In the early days of the twentieth century the copper camps of the southwest were still somewhat untamed. The men who worked the mines were rough in their language and their living. Disagreements were often settled with a weapon or a clenched fist, and on at least one occasion Frank had to put his training as a boxer to use. It is yet another testimony to the hardness of Frank Luke Junior to remember that he was but a teenager during his time in Ajo.

The Arizona territory – raw, arid, and unforgiving, had shaped Frank Junior. His tenure in Ajo and his frequent journeys into the back country had taught him to be resourceful and to take care of himself, for no one was likely to come to his aid should he encounter trouble. Though he was sometimes referred to as quiet and unassuming, he could at once be fiercely loyal and competitive, traits he displayed time and again on the playing fields and in the devotion he showed toward his family and close friends. He also possessed the strong work ethic typical of German immigrant families, along with a streak of stubborn independence.

"At home he was always a good boy," his father said of him, "truthful, steady and industrious."

As he grew up he seemed to develop a strong sense of right and wrong, fair and unfair, and felt a certain affinity for the underdog. At school, he took it upon himself to not only be Bill Elder's friend but also his protector.

On a trip into the Superstitions, Frank once drew a bead on a turkey buzzard that was floating high overhead on the wind currents. Then, thinking the better of it, he lowered his rifle.

"He's not bothering anybody," Frank is said to have muttered.

One also senses that Frank Junior carried with him the sense of invincibility that is common in the young, healthy and strong – and at a most unfortunate moment in history.

Frank Senior, having been an assessor for the Federal Land Bank and a prominent member of the Phoenix business community, embarked upon a successful career in politics. Frank served as the Phoenix City Assessor and later as a Maricopa County Supervisor. At about the time Frank Junior graduated from Phoenix Union High School, Frank Senior moved the family onto a five-acre estate at 2200 West Monroe Street, which at the time was at the very edge of the Phoenix city limits, a stone's throw from where the state capital complex is today in the heart of the sprawling city. The Luke home was a stately nine-bedroom Victorian house that had been built eleven years earlier by a railroad executive and had at one time been home to, of all things, an ostrich farm. Using a system of flood irrigation, the surrounding lawns and pastures were kept green and fertile in the desert heat. The Luke children were put to work keeping the grounds well-manicured and caring for a menagerie of sheep, cows, hogs and chickens. The house on Monroe street became the center of Luke family life but there is little reason to doubt that Frank felt his life calling him; his wanderlust and desire to make something of himself assured that he would not remain there for long.

But in that spring of 1917 events would unfold halfway around the world that would forever alter the destiny of young Frank Luke Junior.

Chapter Two

The horrific world war had been raging for nearly three years, stretching from Russia in the east to the sea lanes of the Atlantic in the west, from the waters surrounding the British Isles as far south as the Horn of Africa. In western Europe the carnage was particularly appalling. Protracted trench warfare was consuming millions of lives; a generation of young European males was being virtually wiped out. Though many Americans condemned the German aggression and sided with the allies, President Woodrow Wilson sought desperately to spare the youth of America from the same fate, adopting a doctrine of neutrality and isolationism.

However, the very oceans that protected the United States were a battleground, and American citizens were continually sailing into harm's way. In their effort to stop the flow of war supplies from the New World, German U-boats sank a number of allied ships upon which Americans traveled. The sinking of the liners *Lusitania* in 1915 and *Laconia* in 1917, resulting in the loss of over 100 American lives, all but evaporated isolationist sentiment in the United States. For a democracy to thrive, seaborne travel and commerce have to continue unabated, and eventually the reckless submarine warfare policies of Germany could no longer be tolerated. The discovery of German attempts to form a military alliance with Mexico against the United States served as a final provocation. On 6 April 1917, Wilson formally asked Congress to declare war.

The government of the United States at once pledged itself to the allied cause, promising a great expeditionary force of fresh troops to reinforce the weary French and British ranks on the

Western Front. All of America was caught up in the rush of patriotism that followed and the feverish preparations for war.

Frank was on another hunting trip with Bill Elder when the United States entered the war. As they rode out of the mountains into the small mining town of Globe, they realized that something had changed – there was an American flag flying proudly from the local brothel.

In the weeks that followed, Frank's brother Edwin enlisted into the Army as an artilleryman. His sister Eva, who joined the Red Cross to begin training as a nurse, encouraged Frank to enlist. His former pastor, Dean Scarlett, recalls that Frank attempted to enlist in the navy, but his induction was delayed due to bout of pleurisy. Frank spent the summer recovering in Phoenix, and afterward decided to apply for a new and very different military branch that appealed to his sense of adventure.

In 1917 the United States was pitifully unprepared for war. Americans had a long held disdain for standing armies, seeing large formations of regular soldiers as potential threats to their personal freedom, preferring a system of state militias as the first line of national defense. While the Navy was able to assist the allies almost immediately, the regular United States Army was a force used for garrisoning frontier outposts and had no regular units larger than a regiment. The Army critically lacked modern weapons, equipment and mechanization. Though the European war was proving the airplane to be indispensable, there was no American air force to speak of. Thousands of recruits would need to be trained, and everything from helmets and gas masks to machine guns, artillery and airplanes would have to be purchased from the already strained war machines of the French and British.

The job of training pilots for these aircraft fell to the new Aviation Section of the U.S. Army Signal Corps. Several American pilots who had volunteered to serve with the British and French air forces were transferred to the U.S. Army, providing a small but valuable core of combat-experienced aviators, and tasked with organizing the fledgling air service. Many of America's most vibrant and brilliant youths, the best she had to offer, queued up for the exciting new opportunity. Many of them were members of the Ivy League elite, for several of the finer eastern universities had flying clubs. Recruiting posters of the day showed a black German vulture cowering before an onrushing Bald Eagle with the legend *Join the Army Air Service! Be an American Eagle!*

Several British and French aviators had already become popular heroes in the United States. The exploits of men like Britain's Albert Ball and France's Georges Guynemer were followed closely by the American wire services. The title of "ace" was bestowed upon a pilot who had shot down five or more enemy aircraft. The aces were often featured in photographs posing beside their machines, handsome men wearing natty tailor-made uniforms with fine knee-length boots and many gleaming medals.

What could be more dashing, roaring into the sky in a sleek pursuit plane to meet the invading Hun in a daring single combat? It seemed so thrilling, so chivalrous and clean, perhaps even *less dangerous*. Americans pored over newspaper stories of the Lafayette Escadrille, a squadron of American volunteers who in 1916 joined the French cause, ostensibly to help repay a debt to France for its part in the American Revolution.

In August of 1917, at the age of 20, Frank journeyed to San Diego, California to enlist in the fledgling Air Service. On his application he applied for commission as a *first* lieutenant, more than likely because he was ignorant of Army rank structure. Frank listed his civilian occupation as "machine inspector, electrolitic [sic] tanks, New Cornelia Copper Company."

How Luke actually gained a commission as an officer is something of a mystery, since he admitted to having only a high school diploma. The Army had already decided that at least some college education was required for pilot training. One supposes that Luke's proclaimed job title, embellished or not, may have led the review board to believe that he had sufficient technical expertise to merit acceptance. He also promised letters of recommendation from the superintendent of public schools in Phoenix, the editor of *The Arizona Gazette* and the Maricopa County treasurer. Following the mental and physical examinations, he was told to return home to await notification of his acceptance for pilot training.

Patience was simply not one of Frank Luke's attributes. Within two weeks he could stand it no longer, and fired off a postcard to the Army. "Kindly let me know when I may expect a call for service," he wrote. Beneath his signature is a quickly scrawled *September 29 Texas*, most likely written by the officer that processed the request, noting where and when Luke was to report for duty...one year to the day before his death.

*   *   *   *

The University of Texas in Austin was the location of the Signal Corps' recently-established School of Military Aeronautics, the first stop for hundreds of new recruits on their way to earning the silver wings of an aviator. SMA, as it was called, was essentially a ground school where the recruits were indoctrinated into military life but devoted the majority of their time to the study of aviation. The eight-week course included lectures on subjects like aerodynamics and navigation, along with practical applications such as the tearing down and reassembling of aircraft engines and machine guns. The recruits were required to properly field-strip and reassemble a machine gun blindfolded while being timed. Luke's time was said to be the fastest.

After completing ground school, Luke returned to Phoenix for a short leave before boarding another train for San Diego. The Signal Corps Aviation School at Rockwell Field was the Army's center for primary flight training, established on the wind-swept sand flats of Coronado Island. It was here that the boy whose high school yearbook said "was too happy-go-lucky to realize his own talents," would soon discover a natural gift.

Even though the Wright Brothers had developed the first successful airplane in the United States more than a decade before, America's commitment to military aviation had been greatly outpaced by other industrialized nations. Despite the promises the Wilson administration made to their new allies, it would be some time before the American aviation industry would be able to produce large numbers of combat aircraft. In fact, only a handful of American-produced planes arrived in France before the Armistice.

To be able to supply front-line squadrons with modern single-seat fighters, the United States purchased a number of planes from the allies, most notably the Nieuport and Spad from France and the Sopwith Camel from Great Britain. Finding it impractical to ship large numbers of these aircraft to the continental U.S. to train their new pilots, the Army established an advanced training depot at Issoudon, France. Frank Luke and his fellow students in San Diego would learn to fly in older Curtis trainers. Once the graduates logged forty hours in the air, they would then be sent to Issoudon to receive further instruction in formation flying and combat tactics, using the same types of fighter aircraft that they would fly once assigned to an operational squadron.

The restless wanderer always in search of adventure soon found a home, and it was in the sky. Luke proved to be a natural pilot, and in December of 1917 was the first in his class to solo. Excitedly he wrote to Albert Pinney and Bill Elder, encouraging them to apply for the Air Service. To strap into the seat of a crafted wood-and-fabric machine trembling with horsepower, to soar high above the sea and the gleaming beaches of southern California, to be the master of machine and of one's destiny...it was a thrill unlike any he had imagined.

Before long, however, Luke showed the first signs of chafing under military discipline. The Curtis Jenny biplanes at Rockwell Field were among the first operational aircraft used by the Army. Aerobatics in the tired old Jennies were forbidden. Frank, it seems, with a certain building confidence as he logged more and more flying time, decided for the first time in his military career to break the rules. It certainly would not be the last time, but it nearly was.

High over Rockwell Field one winter's morning Luke attempted to coax the Curtis he was flying into a loop. The plane gasped and shuddered before finally entering a spin that resembled a falling-leaf pattern. Luke was somehow able to regain control and land safely. It is a testimony to Luke's natural skill as an aviator that he was able to recover from the spin, given that he had very little experience at the time. This may or may not have figured into the base commander's decision to ground him for only three days.

It would be a pattern that would repeat itself many times over the coming months. Flying gave Luke the feeling of freedom for which his restless spirit yearned and he would find it increasingly difficult to strike a balance between the desires of the Army air service and his own.

It was during these demanding and hectic days, when time for leisure and courtship was rare and precious, that Frank began calling on a dark-haired high school senior from San Diego named Marie Rapson. Theirs was a romance of an intensity that could only be experienced in the uncertainty of wartime, and before his tour at Rockwell Field was over the two announced their engagement. The wedding, however, would have to wait. On 23 January 1918 Frank was commissioned a Second Lieutenant in the U.S. Army Air Service and was ordered to New York City to board a transport ship for France.

There would be time, however, for another brief stopover in Phoenix. While staying at the house on Monroe Street, Frank visited family and friends and said his good-byes. Though he was twenty years old, a newly commissioned officer, a pilot, and engaged to be married, Frank could not help but feel a sense of impending doom. To a friend he made the grim prediction that he would not return from France alive.

Chapter Three

Any gloomy intuitions that Frank Luke may have experienced did not seem to dampen his tenacity. On 14 February 1918 the Air Training Signal Office in Washington, D.C. received the following telegram from Rockwell Field:

> OUR TELEGRAM FORTY NINE B OF FEBRUARY FOURTH RECOMMENDED SECOND LIEUTENANT FRANK LUKE JR. AS A BOMBING PILOT. HE WAS ON LEAVE WHEN CLASSIFIED. BOARD HAS RECONSIDERED HIS CASE AND REQUESTS AUTHORITY TO CHANGE HIS CLASSIFICATION FROM BOMBING TO PURSUIT PILOT.

Frank Luke was determined to go where the action was. On 4 March 1918 he boarded the liner *Leviathan* for the trans-Atlantic crossing, landing in the British Isles two weeks later.

"Now, if anything happens to me, I don't want you to feel bad," Frank wrote in a letter to his father. "For you know I have done my duty and enjoy doing it."

By April, after a prolonged stretch of bad weather, he began training at the Third Aviation Instruction Center at Issoudon, France.

At Issoudon the new pilots became accustomed to handling the more advanced pursuit types, learned the subtleties of formation and nap-of-the-earth flying and received briefings in air-to-air battle tactics from more experienced combat pilots.

"Oh, boy, it's great to be up flying, practicing stunts, and looking down on the earth spread out beneath you," Luke wrote to Bill Elder.

"His progress through this school was discouraging," the adjutant of the Issoudon base wrote in an Army memo. One wonders if these comments are meant to describe Luke's straining under the bridle of Army discipline rather than his proficiency as an aviator. His personal journal describes praise from his instructors, including Quentin Roosevelt. Other accounts of those who remember him claim that he was an able pilot and a first-rate marksman, two abilities critical for success (and survival) rarely found in one person.

However, beginning with a harrowing episode on 1 May 1918, Luke experienced a string of unfortunate mishaps. One could argue that a lesser pilot would not have survived.

High above the French countryside Luke was practicing vertical spirals, on each maneuver he attempted to push the aircraft higher and closer to a ninety degrees angle of climb. During one of these maneuvers he spiraled upward to three thousand feet but lost control of the ship as it began to descend. The plane jerked violently, his safety belt became unfastened, and Luke was nearly thrown from the cockpit.

"I caught the upper wing with my left hand and saved myself," Luke wrote in his diary. He ended up on the floor of the cockpit as the aircraft plunged earthward "at a terrific speed."

Luke pushed himself back into the seat and fought with the controls, realizing that he had already dropped nearly 1000 feet. After several attempts to regain control had failed and the airplane's downward velocity increased, Luke began to think he was doomed. Finally Luke was able to recover from the spin, level off at just over 100 feet, and bring the plane in for a landing.

Safely back on the ground, Luke watched as ground crewmen, motorcycles and ambulances raced over from the aerodrome. The ground crew believed that Luke had crashed. One of them remarked that watching the whole event had made him physically sick.

Any landing that you can walk away from is a good one, so the aviator's saying goes.

After dropping out of formations, running out of fuel during a training mission, and on another occasion making a forced landing in a French garden patch, Luke was retained in training longer than most. He was sent to the airfield at Cazau for further instruction before finally being assigned to a duty station.

Much to Luke's dismay, rather than being assigned to a combat squadron he was sent to the replacement pool at Orly airport outside of Paris. At Orly, new aircraft from French and British factories were put through test flights before being accepted for use by the American forces. In June of 1918, while the soldiers and Marines of the American Expeditionary Force were engaged in savage fighting at Belleau Wood and Chateau Thierry, Frank was put to work ferrying replacement airplanes to front-line squadrons. It was dull and thankless work, and though he became increasingly frustrated at being kept out of combat, he no doubt benefited from the extra flight experience.

On 20 July 1918, a flight of five pursuit planes from the 27th Aero Squadron based at Saintes took off on an offensive patrol over the German lines. In the previous four days, the 27th had lost one pilot killed in action, one severely wounded, and another forced down behind enemy lines and captured.

On this day the patrol ran into an enemy formation over Soissons. Though the Americans claimed two German fighters were destroyed in the action, two American aircraft were lost behind enemy lines, both pilots severely wounded and taken prisoner. A third pilot, First Lieutenant Fred Norton, crashed within the American lines and died in the hospital three days later.

On 25 July 1918, Frank Luke was assigned as a replacement pilot to the 27th Aero Squadron.

*   *   *   *

The first airplanes used in the Great War were not used for combat, but for observation. In the first days of the conflict, awkward and primitive-looking two-seater biplanes would float above the battle lines, their observers plotting and photographing enemy positions.

In the four years following 1914, military aviation evolved at a breakneck pace. Synchronization gear was developed that allowed machine guns to be mounted to a plane's engine cowling and fired through the spinning propeller. Single-seat pursuit planes were developed, so named because their purpose was to chase down observation planes and destroy them before the vital information they collected could be relayed to enemy generals.

With every change of season, both sides produced new models of combat aircraft; each faster, more maneuverable, and more deadly than the last. Pursuit pilots would not only hunt reconnaissance planes but would attack observation balloons, enemy troop formations, gun emplacements...and each other. By 1916 British and French squadrons were tangling with German

Jagdgeschwaders, so called "Flying Circuses" of up to fifty aircraft. During these massive "dogfights" the sky would be filled with swirling, diving, shooting -- and burning -- pursuit planes.

It was no longer a glamorous proposition. Combat in the skies above France was proving to be as deadly as any other sort. Shattered by explosive bullets, planes would spin out of control or erupt into flames, their fragile wings tearing away as they plummeted earthward. Parachutes, armor plating, self-sealing fuel tanks and other features meant to offer the pilot a measure of survivability were still in the experimental stage or yet to be invented. Contrary to Hollywood legend, there was little room for chivalry. The pilots of World War One fought to the death. The best way to shoot down an enemy plane, American ace Eddie Rickenbacker admitted, was to shoot the other pilot in the back.

By July of 1918, the young Americans of the 27th Aero Squadron were finding that the great adventure that they had signed-on for was in fact a very deadly one. Major Harold E. Hartney already knew this.

Hartney was actually Canadian, seconded to the U.S. Air Service by the Royal Flying Corps, to help staff the new American squadrons with veteran combat pilots. In his previous tour of duty Hartney had already had several brushes with death; in February of 1917 he survived a crash after being shot down by Manfred von Richtofen, the infamous Red Baron. Hartney had become an ace, destroying five German airplanes in air-to-air combat, before assuming command of the 27th Aero Squadron. He did his best to pass hard-earned wisdom on to his new American colleagues. Though small in stature, Hartney possessed a commanding presence, and his confidence and teaching ability earned him the respect of his younger charges.

Hartney's 27th was quartered with two other squadrons of the First Pursuit Group at an airfield outside of the French village of

Saintes. The airfield was a sodden patch of beaten ground, heavily rutted by the constant churning of airplane and truck tires. In most of the period photographs of Saintes the dominant feature is mud, a thick wet porridge liberally splattered across airplane fuselages, canvas flaps of temporary hangars and clinging heavily to boots. Here and there patches of tortured grass struggled to survive. Drab, hastily-erected structures provided offices, mess halls and shelter for aircraft and their overworked ground crews. The pilots themselves were quartered at a shoddy former hotel in the village.

Ten green replacement pilots arrived at the adjutant's office of the First Pursuit Group on 25 July, among them was Frank Luke Junior. Six of the new pilots, including Luke, were assigned to the hard-luck 27th Aero Squadron.

The next morning, the six replacements dressed and shaved and reported to the airfield, where they stood in formation outside of the squadron offices. Major Hartney emerged from the building, took his place before the group of newcomers standing stiffly at attention, and delivered a blunt "welcome" speech.

"You are in the 27th in name only. When you have shown your buddies out there that you have guts and can play the game honestly and courageously, they'll probably let you stay. You'll know without my telling you when you are actually members of this gang. It's up to you.

"If you survive the first two weeks you're well over the hill. I'm not trying to discourage any of you, but you may as well know what you're up against from the first. Some of you are certain to be washed out during the first two weeks. If you get through that period safely and your own personal god continues to strap himself in with you, you'll probably accomplish things. That's all, gentlemen."

As the formation was dismissed, Hartney noticed a lean, blond kid in the ranks staring back at him. Hartney had met

Frank Luke Junior the day before and had perused his log book, noting that the boy's appearance pretty much matched the reputation that preceded him. Luke was the one that everybody at Issoudon was talking about, the arrogant cowboy spoiling for a fight, the one who was supposed to be a hotshot pilot and marksman, the loud-mouth who all but claimed he would whip the Huns single-handed once given the chance.

Luke was grinning at him.

"He seemed to be saying, *don't kid me...I'm not afraid of the bogeyman*," Hartney remembered.

In the same formation was another young lieutenant. He was tall, slender and dark-haired with a pair of troubled brown eyes and a stern dimpled chin. His name was Joseph F. Wehner.

* * * *

The fervent tide of patriotism that swept across the United States following its entry into the First World War produced a most unfortunate and hateful byproduct. Hundreds of thousands of Germans had immigrated to the United States in the previous century, becoming loyal citizens and productive members of their communities, serving as able artisans, farmers, industrialists and businessmen. When the war in Europe began, many voiced support for the isolationist movement, hoping to avoid going to war against their native country.

Twenty years earlier, stories printed by eastern newspaper tabloids had Americans clamoring for war against Spain. In 1917, the same newspapers substituted the word *German* with degrading terms such as *Hun* and printed vivid accounts, both real and imagined, of German atrocities against French and Belgian civilians. Commercial artists capitalized on these news items when drawing recruiting posters, depicting German soldiers as barbaric killers of women and children. Their work encouraged many to enlist but also fueled discrimination against German-Americans.

In a speech delivered in New York City in November of 1917, former American ambassador to Germany James Gerard Watson said, "If there are any German-Americans here, that are so ungrateful for all the benefits that they have received that they are still for the Kaiser, there is only one thing to do with them, and that is to hog tie them, give them back the wooden shoes and rags they landed in, and ship them back to the Fatherland."

German immigrants, many of them fiercely loyal Americans, were looked upon with suspicion and distrust and taunted in the workplace and in their neighborhoods. There was widespread belief, encouraged by the Kaiser's propaganda machine, that German-Americans would rise up in an armed revolt to wreak havoc within the United States.

The problem worsened with the passage of the Sedition Act of 1918, which specifically targeted German-Americans and allowed prosecution for anyone who "shall willfully utter, print, write, or publish any disloyal, profane, scurrilous, or abusive language about the form of government of the United States." Federal agents censored German-American newspapers, closed German language schools and banned German-American theater and literature.

Just prior to America entering the war, Edward V. "Eddie" Rickenbacher, a popular race car driver, endured such discrimination at home and was even tailed by Scotland Yard detectives during a business trip to Great Britain. Rickenbacher, who would eventually become America's top-scoring fighter ace, a squadron commander and Medal of Honor recipient, was confined to his ship when it docked in England. Even the good-natured Eddie (who thought the whole episode was quite humorous) would later succumb to anti-German sentiment and change the spelling of his surname to Rickenbacker. A newspaper reporter noticed and wrote an article under the headline *Eddie Rickenbacker takes the Hun out of his name.*

The suspicions of allied authorities were not entirely groundless. Much of the success of the German submarine campaign could be attributed to their intelligence apparatus. German U-boats were sinking a great number of allied merchant ships, threatening to put a stranglehold on the flow of critically needed war materiel. As the airplane grew into prominence as a weapon of war, German agents turned their attention to the Allied air forces.

American Robert M. Todd, a Sopwith Camel pilot with the 17th Aero Squadron, was forced down behind enemy lines and captured in the summer of 1918. Todd was astonished at how much his German interrogators knew about his squadron, including the names of several key officers and where they fit into the unit's table of organization. The flamboyant French ace

Charles Nungesser was reputed to be a frequent bedfellow of the notorious Mata Hari, the exotic dancer and seductress later caught spying for the Germans.

Many young Americans of German descent enlisted willfully to affirm their allegiance to the United States, only to be regarded with suspicion by their fellow soldiers. One of them was Joe Wehner.

Wehner grew up the son of a humble shoemaker in Everette, Massachusetts, just outside of Boston. Like Frank Luke, he excelled on the football gridiron and won a scholarship to Phillips Exeter Academy, a prestigious prep school in New Hampshire. After graduation, Joe traveled to Berlin as an employee of the YMCA, which was engaged in assisting allied prisoners of war. When the United States broke off diplomatic relations with Germany in the spring of 1917, Wehner was repatriated along with other American aid workers and diplomats.

Eager to serve his country and profess his loyalty, Joe enlisted in the Army immediately upon his return to the United States and was accepted for pilot training in the Signal Corps. When word of his Berlin connection reached his superiors, they contacted the Justice Department. An investigation determined that Wehner was not engaged in any subversive activity. Before he departed for France, Wehner would be detained by the Secret Service and investigated a second time before being cleared of any wrongdoing.

But the damage was already done, and Joe's reputation as a suspected German spy preceded him to Issoudon and to Saintes, where on 25 July 1918 he was assigned to the 27th Aero Squadron of the First Pursuit Group, the same day as Frank Luke. Like Frank Luke, Wehner was labeled an outcast by his fellow pilots almost immediately.

It seemed that everywhere he went, Joe was subject to sidelong glances and whispered musings. Sometimes their contempt was more openly displayed, like when they nicknamed him "Fritz." This may not seem like much of a slight today, but during the First World War "Fritz" was the nickname that Americans assigned to the common German soldier, much like "Charlie" was the nickname given to the enemy in Viet Nam.

These two young men would soon find that they shared common ground. They were the two black sheep of their newfound military family: Frank the boastful redneck, Joe the alleged spy. The two had to endure the distrust and disdain of their peers at the same time that they faced their first forays into combat and the prospect of an early death. In such shared adversity strong friendships are formed, and theirs was no exception.

Both were eager to prove themselves as warriors; Joe, because he was a loyal American; Frank, because he knew he was truly capable of doing what he claimed.

Their partnership would become what could only be described as legendary, the type of bond found only between men who have trusted one another with their lives.

Together they would make history.

Frank Luke Jr. posing in front of his Spad XIII at Rembercourt aerodrome, September 1918 (Arizona Historical Society)

Frank Luke Jr., newly-commissioned Second Lieutenant and aviator, January 1918 (USAF)

First Lieutenant Joseph F. Wehner, Luke's trusted friend and flying partner. (USAF)

Major Harold Hartney, commanding officer of the 27th Aero Squadron and later the First Pursuit Group, who became Luke's mentor (USAF)

Captain Jerry Vasconcelles, the popular, practical-joking flight leader and ace with 6 aerial victories. (USAF)

Army Air Service recruiting poster, mentioned in text. (Rosebud Archive)

Eddie Rickenbacker, America's top fighter ace with 26 victories, with his Nieuport N.28 (USAF)

Colonel Billy Mitchell, chief of air service units for the U.S. First Army (left) with Eddie Rickenbacker. (USAF)

Frank Luke Junior beside the wreckage of the German Halberstadt observation aircraft that he shot down on 18 September 1918. The immense sadness that Frank experienced is evident on his face in these photographs, taken just after the death of his close friend Joe Wehner. (Rosebud Archive)

Captain Alfred Grant, who succeeded Hartney as commanding officer of the 27th Aero Squadron. Though Grant and Luke had a tumultuous relationship, it was Grant who wrote the recommendation for Luke's Medal of Honor. (USAF)

A German observation balloon. (Rosebud Archive)

Another *Drachen* is readied for service somewhere in France. (Rosebud Archive)

A *Drachen* operating over France in World War One, as seen from an attacker's point of view. Note gondola slung beneath the balloon and antiaircraft gun emplacements at lower right. (Rosebud Archive)

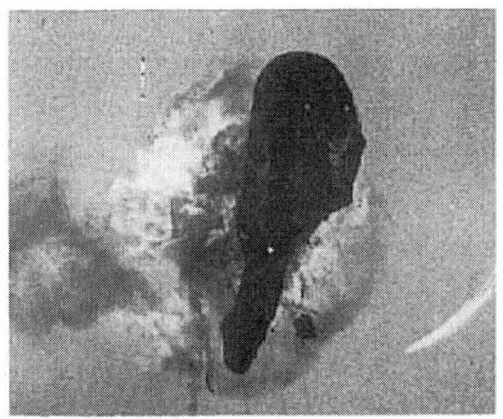

A hydrogen gas-filled observation balloon burns furiously after being attacked by Allied aircraft (Rosebud Archive)

A Fokker D-7, Germany's premier fighter aircraft of late 1918 (Rosebud Archive)

The area where Frank Luke landed on September 29, 1918. The village of Murvaux can be seen in the distance, the trees along Milly Creek where he made his final stand can be seen on the left. (Photo by the author).

The village of Murvaux as it appears today. (Photo by the author.)

The Meuse River valley as it appears today, where Luke saw the majority of his combat. (Photo by the author)

The final resting place of Second Lieutenant Frank Luke Junior at the Meuse-Argonne American Cemetery in Romagne, France. (Photo by the author.)

Chapter Four

Despite the losses sustained and the number of inexperienced men on the roster, the 27th Aero Squadron was still expected to fly offensive patrols and escort allied observation planes on missions over the German lines.

Luke was put to work almost immediately. After listening to Major Hartney's speech, he was assigned a Nieuport scout plane and along with four other pilots practiced formation flying well within the comparative safety of the American lines. Hartney insisted that his men keep a tight formation; it allowed the pilots to watch over and support one another if attacked. Simply put, there was safety in numbers.

That afternoon, Frank participated in his first patrol near the front. Hartney, Alfred Grant, Jerry Vasconcelles and other experienced men formed a protective screen around the rookies and gave them an aerial tour of the sector. For the first time the men saw the snaking trench lines that ran like a gray festering scar across the green plains of eastern France. No enemy aircraft were encountered and all of the Nieuports returned without incident.

When the unpredictable French weather allowed it, Luke flew more combat patrols over the next week, each as uneventful as the last and always under the watchful eyes of a more experienced squadron mate. For Luke, his chief purpose during these first patrols was familiarization, to be able to recognize landmarks in the sector and find his way back to the airfield should he become separated from the flock. When not on patrol, he continued to practice formation flying and learned combat tactics under the tutelage of Harold Hartney.

A common problem with pilots new to the front was what fliers called "air blindness," an inability to visually acquire other aircraft in the surrounding sky. This deadly shortcoming was usually corrected with experience, but there was little time to gain any. Hartney took the new pilots under his wing, so to speak, and harangued them to constantly scan the sky in every direction and not be lulled into inattention by the scenery and the droning of the aircraft motor. He taught them to always watch for an unexpected enemy coming out of the sun and to attack in the same fashion whenever possible. After a few short days the new boys were expected to take an active part in squadron operations, and hopefully survive.

When Luke arrived at Saintes, the 27th Squadron was in the process of transitioning from the dainty Nieuport scout to the more rugged Spad XIII. The Spad was a stubby, snub-nosed bulldog of an airplane. Though not as agile as the Nieuport or the British Sopwith Camel, the Spad was very fast for its time. It could out-dive most of its opponents and had an impressive rate of climb. Many American pilots favored the Spad for these reasons while others (including Hartney) hated to see the Nieuports go.

The name *Spad* was an acronym for the French manufacturer, the Société Anonyme Pour L'Aviation et ses Dérives. The Spad was powered by a 235-horsepower liquid-cooled Hispano-Suiza 8 cylinder engine, which the pilots referred to as a Hisso. Two fixed British Vickers .303-caliber machine guns were mounted in front of the cockpit and synchronized to fire through the propeller. Unlike the Nieuport, which had the nasty habit of shedding its fabric wing covering during the stress of combat, the Spad had a sturdy airframe could absorb a lot of abuse. Both the Hisso and the Vickers guns, however, were temperamental pieces of equipment.

The Spads were painted in muted olive and khaki camouflage, with red-white-and-blue markings known as roundels, similar to a bulls-eye, on the wing tips to identify thcm as American. This was adapted from the British and French, who used similar markings with the colors displayed in a different order. After the war America would choose a more distinct white star for the national symbol on its airplanes.

To these standard markings the 27th Aero Squadron added some personal touches. The nose of each Spad was painted royal blue. A Bald Eagle, its wings outstretched and framed by a blazing red sun, adorned both sides of the Spad fuselage. Taking their cue from the French, the Americans developed unit names and emblems for their pursuit squadrons, the most famous of which was probably Rickenbacker's Hat-in-the-Ring Squadron. Hartney's band became known as the Eagle Squadron.

In early August, the First Pursuit Group continued to use the familiar Nieuports for combat missions while both pilots and maintenance crews became accustomed to the new Spads. Luke had logged many hours in the Nieuport as a ferry pilot and during his familiarization patrols.

A pursuit squadron becomes a close-knit cadre. The pilots of the 27th had been stung by the losses of recent days, but what happened on 1 August 1918 was even worse.

Eighteen planes from the Eagle Squadron took off from Saintes to provide protection for a flight of two-seater reconnaissance aircraft. Luke's motor began giving him trouble and he was forced to return to the airfield. Along with other pilots who had similar maintenance problems, he waited anxiously for the squadron to return from its mission. After an hour or so they started coming back to the airfield in singles and in pairs, indicating that they had been dispersed by combat. Here and there the Nieuports bore the scars of battle: a piece of torn fabric flapping in the wind, a splintered wing strut, a fuselage stitched by a half-dozen Maxim slugs.

High over the tiny village of Fere-en-Tardenois, the patrol had run headlong into *Jagdgeschwader 1*, the Red Baron's Flying Circus.

A fierce and deadly dogfight had ensued. Three members of the 27th were killed outright and three others who crashed behind enemy lines were captured. Among them was Lt. Arthur Whiton, one of the new pilots who joined the squadron the same day as Luke.

Although the Americans were able to gun-down five of the attacking German Fokker D-7s, there was little cause for celebration. They had lost six more of their own. Six bright young men, each face clearly etched in the minds of the survivors. They were friends with whom they shared quarters. The same guys with whom they played pickup football games. They had shared jokes only a few hours earlier over the breakfast table.

The events of this awful day almost certainly contributed to the contempt the men of the Eagle Squadron held for Frank Luke Junior.

According to Hartney, Luke seemed to be shy and did not participate in the banter at the officer's mess. "It unquestionably caused him many heartburns when his reticence was interpreted as conceit," Hartney later wrote.

"A lot of people were put off by him at the outset," Frank Junior's nephew Don Luke told the author in 2012. "That caused him to go off on his own. If there was arrogance, it came mostly from being twenty-one."

When Luke did talk, it was usually about flying into combat and the expectations that he had for himself. Frank truly believed in his ability both as a pilot and a hunter, and simply knew that he would be successful.

Many of the pilots who enlisted in the Air Service hailed from the campuses of Ivy League colleges, and their brand of fraternity house humor was not easy for an Arizona copper miner to understand. To say that he had trouble fitting-in would be a gross understatement.

Frank kept to himself, spending much of his time in extensive practice sessions on the machine gun range and tinkering with his aircraft motor. In actuality, he had more in common with the mechanics out in the maintenance sheds than with his fellow aviators in the officer's mess.

One story about Luke spread like wildfire through the squadron. It occurred on the day an enemy plane appeared over the airfield.

"That would be a cinch for me," Luke remarked to a sergeant standing next to him.

To a group of fighter pilots who faced real combat and had recently watched several of their friends die, this kind of cockiness was hard to take. Who did this hick from Arizona think he was? What the hell did *he* know about combat?

Two weeks later, the men of the Eagle Squadron would change their opinion. They would stop calling Frank Luke a braggart and start calling him a downright liar.

* * * *

Mercifully, the foul weather and the transition into Spads offered a short respite from combat. Major Hartney used the interval to perform some sorely needed training for the newer pilots. The squadron commander hammered home the basics of dogfighting: always try to gain altitude over the opponent, when attacked from behind break sharply to one side and do not dive, always watch for the decoy and the trap.

Luke's respect for Hartney was growing steadily and he listened intently to the older man's lessons. One day Hartney and Luke drove to the front lines near Fere-en-Tardenois to view the wreckage of downed aircraft that were scattered across the battlefield. Luke noted that several of the wrecked planes had bullet holes through the headrest of the pilot's seat, an indication that the flier had tried to shake his pursuer by diving instead of turning away. Hartney knew what he was talking about. On their way back to Saintes, Luke and Hartney watched as a German Albatross fighter roared through a hail of gunfire to destroy an Allied observation balloon. The incident, Hartney knew, made quite an impression on the young aviator.

Like the rest of the Eagle Squadron, Hartney believed that Luke was exasperatingly arrogant, but couldn't help liking him a little. Hartney had begun his military career as an infantry officer in the Canadian militia, serving in the western reaches of

Saskatchewan. The regiment was made up of tough youngsters from the wilds of the Canadian frontier, and this experience helped him to understand Frank Luke. In his memoirs, Hartney echoed the sentiments of George Washington: when commanding those who are "individualists, who have always done their own thinking, they cannot be successfully driven. They must be led." Frank Luke Junior was an individualist if there ever was one.

In time Hartney would become Luke's trusted confidant and supporter. For this the brash young pilots sarcastically referred to Luke as "Hartney's boyfriend."

On the evening of 16 August 1918, Hartney led a group of Spads on a mission to escort a flight of reconnaissance aircraft over the German lines. The patrol got off to a very bad start.

The Hisso engines installed in the Spads were proving to be extremely troublesome. As the patrol struggled to get airborne, a

Spad piloted by Lt. Ruliff Nevius staggered and crashed, killing Nevius in the process.

Luke's Hisso ran poorly before he ever left the ground and he spent an hour with the squadron mechanics fixing the errant motor before taking off to find the formation.

Luke and Nevius were not the only ones to have engine trouble that day. One by one Spads dropped from Major Hartney's formation, returning to the safety of the American lines, their motors chugging roughly. An intensely irritated Hartney headed for the advanced airfield at Coincy. He found nearly all of the Spads from his patrol there, being worked on by mechanics. Like Hartney, the pilots were frustrated with the Spads and they uttered choice words about the French and American brass who had taken away their beloved Nieuports.

As Hartney taxied to a stop, another Spad banked over the field and came in for a landing. It was Luke. The pilots gathered beside Hartney's plane and watched. One of them remarked that Luke had been bragging that today he would bag his first German.

Sure enough, Luke claimed that he had shot down a German plane.

"I got me a Hun," Luke told Hartney.

Frank's squadron mates snorted with disgust, and Hartney asked him where the action had occurred. Luke stated he wasn't sure, he thought it was somewhere near Soissons.

According to his official report, Luke left the aerodrome to try to catch up with Hartney's flight but could not find them. Over the German lines he spotted a loose formation of Fokkers and climbed into the sun to get above them. Luke stated that he cut his motor and dove on the rearmost German fighter, closing to a distance of 100 feet before restarting the engine and opening up with his twin Vickers guns.

Luke claimed that he got as close to the German as he dared and continued to fire his machine guns before finally peeling off and making a run for the allied lines. Luke watched the German aircraft roll onto its back and spin earthward, and was almost certain that it crashed. On his way to Coincy Luke said that he ran across four other German planes but did not engage them.

Other reports filed for 16 August state that the atmosphere that day was heavy with ground haze, and no other allied fliers or observation crews could confirm Luke's claim. Some accounts state that Hartney confirmed the claim and the kill was credited to Luke, but both Hartney and the official history of the First Pursuit Group record the victory as unconfirmed.

For the aviators of the Eagle Squadron, Luke's dubious claim was more than they were willing to stand. Using the parlance of the age, they quickly labeled him a "four flusher" – that is, a liar – and the gulf between Frank and his fellow officers widened immensely. Some of the longer-standing members began approaching Hartney with proposals to have Luke transferred out of the squadron. When Joe Wehner expressed his belief in Luke's claim, "Fritz" also became an object of their hostility.

Rather than toasting Luke's first victory, Hartney grounded him for three days for his unauthorized solo mission and ordered him to stand a continuous sixteen-hour watch as the duty officer.

Luke resolved that his next victory would not go uncounted.

Chapter Five

The latter half of August 1918 was a busy time for the Eagle Squadron. The United States First Army began plans for the first major offensive by American troops in the war. The objective was to reduce a salient in the front lines near the town of Saint Mihiel. A salient, or forward bulge in the battle line, is usually seen as a tactical liability, since the forces that occupy it are constantly under threat of being attacked on their flanks and surrounded. The Germans, however, had worked hard to maintain and fortify the Saint Mihiel salient since the opening months of the war in order to interrupt the east-west lines of the French railway system and thus make it difficult for the Allies to keep their forces resupplied along the entire front.

The Allied attack was set for 12 September and would involve some 300,000 American soldiers and Marines along with 110,000 French troops. The objective would be to roll back the salient and hopefully cut-off and destroy the weary German army that was occupying it.

The Saint Mihiel offensive would also be one of the earliest examples of infantry advancing with support from tanks, and of American combat aircraft providing close-air support for ground forces in the attack. Over a thousand allied aircraft were put to the task, under the command of Colonel William Mitchell, the air commander for General John Pershing's First Army.

In preparation for the offensive, Mitchell ordered the First Pursuit Group to relocate to new airfields closer to the front line. The 27th Aero Squadron would move to the village of Rembercourt. The airfield there was meticulously camouflaged and movements of aircraft and equipment were carefully planned to avoid detection by the enemy.

By the time the move was complete, the 27th would have a new commanding officer. Colonel Mitchell selected Harold Hartney to command the First Pursuit Group and coordinate the efforts of its four squadrons during the offensive. Replacing Hartney at the helm of the Eagle Squadron would be Captain Alfred A. Grant. On 21 August 1918, Grant assumed command of the unit.

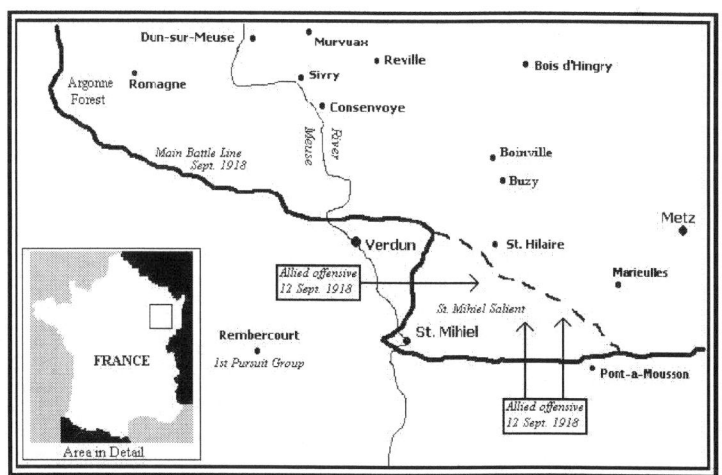

Grant had a very different style of leadership than that of Harold Hartney. A member of the cadet corps in college, he insisted on military correctness, discipline and strict adherence to regulations. If Hartney was the popular coach in the school of aerial combat, Grant was the stern headmaster. An original member of the 27th Squadron, Grant was present during Luke's earliest days in the unit and shared the same opinion of the Arizonan held by the majority of the squadron. To Luke, things could not have been worse. It would only be a matter of time before Grant and Luke butted heads.

On 1 September 1918 the squadron finished its move to the new aerodrome at Rembercourt and began receiving a new crop of replacement pilots to bring the roster up to full strength. On the evening of 11 September, while hundreds of thousands of allied soldiers prepared to attack the next day, the pilots of the First

Pursuit Group gathered in the officer's mess and discussed their part in the coming offensive.

"The Air Service will take the offensive at all points with the objective of destroying the enemy's air service, attacking his troops on the ground and protecting our own air and ground troops," the operations order stated. The First Pursuit Group was to provide direct support to the First Army in the Saint Mihiel region and "attack hostile balloon positions at the same time protecting all allied reconnaissance operating in the sector."

Observation balloons, called *Drachens* by the Germans and nicknamed "sausages" by the allies, became the focus of conversation. Used extensively by both sides during the war, the balloons were set-up just behind the front lines to gather reconnaissance information, and were highly effective in their task. When an enemy balloon was aloft nearby, any overt movement was sure to draw a barrage of accurate artillery and mortar fire. Needless to say, everyone from field marshals down to infantry privates hated the things. A First World War expression still in use today in America's military is "the balloon's gone up," which means something bad is about to happen.

The great oblong canvas bags were filled with highly-volatile hydrogen gas to make them lighter than air. A gondola was slung beneath the balloon with enough space for two trained observers and their communications equipment. The balloons were tethered by two-thousand-foot steel cables, operated by large winches mounted to flatbed trucks.

Observation balloons were not easy targets. Both sides placed a high value on the balloons, both militarily and financially, and went to great lengths to protect them from attack.

The balloons were surrounded by multiple layers of antiaircraft defense, from heavy machine guns to rapid-fire cannon and mortars. The known altitude of the balloon made range-finding quite accurate and allowed the gunners to throw a veritable curtain of lead into the face of an attacking pursuit pilot. In most cases, the observers had machine guns swivel-mounted on the edge of the gondola basket to aid in their defense. The balloons were further protected by relays of enemy fighters circling high overhead, ready to pounce on any would-be attacker.

Firing at the balloon from a safe distance was not an option for the attacker. Both the range and firepower of World War One-era light machine guns of the type used on pursuit aircraft were limited, requiring the attacking pilot to get quite close to the "sausage" in order to hit it with enough incendiary ammunition to set it on fire. If the balloon exploded, the pilot had to work fast to avoid being engulfed in the fireball.

An attack on an observation balloon was, therefore, often considered a suicide mission.

"Anyone who shoots down a balloon has my respect," ace pilot Jerry Vasconcelles remarked that night. The other veterans nodded in agreement. In one corner of the room, listening silently, were Frank Luke and Joe Wehner.

*   *   *   *

The twelfth day of September was an important one for the soldiers of the American Expeditionary Force. Preparations for the Saint Mihiel offensive had been made in painstaking detail. Pershing had promised the French that the German salient would be rolled back in less than a week. While the Americans had performed well in previous defensive actions, the credibility of the United States as a military power rested on this one attack. Everyone from Pershing down to the doughboys in the trenches (and the pilots in their concealed aerodromes) felt the pressure to perform.

Before dawn, the First Pursuit pilots at Rembercourt heard the allied artillery begin a massive preparatory barrage. Dark clouds hung low in the morning sky and soon a heavy downpour added to the misery. The first patrol scheduled for six o'clock was grounded due to the lousy weather. To the east the sounds of artillery rumbled and rolled along with the thunderstorm as the attack got underway. Just after seven a.m. the rain began to slacken.

Eight Spads were rolled out onto the muddy field and a force of grimy mechanics, riggers and armorers pored over the ships, making their last-minute checks. Joe Wehner was standing by his plane when Frank Luke sidled up alongside him.

"Remember what Vasconcelles said last night about attacking balloons?" he asked.

"Yeah," Wehner replied. "Why?"

"I'm going to get a balloon today," Luke said confidently.

The ground crewmen exchanged glances, and after the Spads lifted off the soggy field and headed toward the front, various versions of Luke's remark made the rounds.

So the cowboy is at it again, the pilots said to one another. More Power To You, they said, sarcastically invoking the squadron motto. If he had the guts to actually try, which was doubtful, they had surely seen the last of the Arizona Boaster.

The inclement weather had made a shambles of the morning flight schedule. Anxious to get off the ground and start the show, the young lieutenants piloting the Spads of the Eagle Squadron scattered to the four winds.

Luke left Rembercourt and headed almost due east toward the village of Lavigneville. As he neared the battle line, he spotted three enemy aircraft in the sky ahead and gave chase. Near the town of Pont-a-Mousson and the southernmost shoulder of the salient, the fleeing Germans turned north toward the larger city of Metz, entered a bank of clouds, and gave him the slip.

Undaunted, Luke continued north and flew over the battle raging far below, crossing into German territory. As he neared the smashed, rubble-strewn village of Marieulles, Luke spotted what he was looking for, bobbing on its tether beneath the rain clouds.

It was a *Drachen*.

Remembering what Hartney had taught him, Luke put the Spad into a steady climb and scanned the sky for enemy fighters before swooping in for the kill. Luke nosed the Spad into a steep dive, his Vickers guns chattering.

Immediately the sky around him began filling with the black bursts of exploding antiaircraft shells. Large incendiary rounds that looked like flaming tennis balls zipped past, and streams of machine gun tracer bullets reached out for him. The German ground crew scrambled for the winch controls and started reeling the balloon earthward.

Luke kept firing, holding the screaming Spad in a dive for as long as he dared. Finally he eased back on the stick, cranked into a fast turn and made another pass. The balloon jerked awkwardly at the end of its tether as the winch worked to save it. Luke's guns stuttered and went silent. A feed jam.

Luke zoomed away, reaching forward to try to free the actions of the two Vickers guns. The right gun remained jammed but he was able to get the left one functioning. Once again Frank turned toward the balloon and started another run. The sausage was nearing the ground and the enemy gunners were blazing away with everything they had. Luke pressed the trigger and fired a final burst. The observer, a young officer named Willi Klemm, slumped in the gondola. One of Frank's bullets had lanced through his chest, killing him instantly.

Suddenly, there was a terrific explosion as the balloon burst into flames and dropped into a burning mass on top of the winch. The Spad turned away from the withering antiaircraft fire and zoomed for the American lines.

* * * *

On the western side of the battle line, the American air service had set up its own observation balloons to keep watch over the attack, which so far was going well. The soldiers that formed one of the balloon crews looked skyward when they heard a droning Hisso and saw a shot-up Spad angling down for a landing in a nearby field.

Lieutenant Joseph M. Fox watched as a lean, blond youth emerged from the cockpit of the Spad and asked if he had seen the German balloon catch fire near Marieulles.

Sure, Fox replied, it was hard to miss. He added that there were probably a good number of Huns killed when the balloon exploded so close to the ground.

Fox watched as Frank Luke produced a pen and scratched out the details of the event on a blank affidavit that he had typed out especially for the purpose of confirming an aerial victory. Luke asked Fox and another witness to sign the document, thanked the balloon observers and headed for his Spad. The fighter staggered across the field, the engine sputtering. The Hisso had been damaged by enemy fire and would go no further.

Frank spent the night with the balloon company and in the morning hitched a ride back to Rembercourt in the sidecar of a motorcycle. Frank Luke, his face unshaven and smoke-stained and his flying suit splattered with mud, reported to Grant's office and handed over the signed statement that confirmed his first kill.

When they were finally able to get Luke's plane back to Rembercourt, the maintenance chief shook his head. The Spad was shot full of holes. It was a wonder that Luke wasn't full of holes, the chief told him.

Frank just laughed. "They can't get me," he said.

Chapter Six

By the third day it was evident that Pershing's attack was going to be a rout. Intelligence estimates claiming that German forces in the Saint Mihiel region were strained to the breaking point had proved to be correct. Within hours, the Germans were forced to withdraw from territory that had cost them many days of hard fighting and many thousands of lives. By 14 September 1918, although they had also suffered heavy casualties, the Americans were rounding up scores of German prisoners.

The coordinated aerial assault was also proving to be a success. On the second and third days of the offensive, the squadrons of the First Pursuit Group ventured deeper into German territory to attack the retreating enemy columns and thwart any effort to re-group and counterattack. Killing observation balloons remained a top priority.

On the morning of 14 September, a formation of twelve Spads of the Eagle Squadron departed the Rembercourt airfield and headed east. The battle plan was for designated "shooters" to drop out of formation and attack observation balloons while the remaining Spads kept watch for prowling enemy fighters. The left guns of the shooters were loaded entirely with phosphorous tracer ammunition for igniting balloons. Frank Luke was one of the shooters.

Luke's victory two days earlier, and the manner in which he had confirmed it, did little to enhance his reputation. While it did raise some eyebrows, most felt that a Frank Luke without any kills to his credit was bad enough. A Frank Luke with confirmed victories would be insufferable.

Still, the members of the Eagle Squadron had to have been questioning their initial impressions. They had not forgotten Luke's outrageous claim of 15 August, and he had been getting rather chummy lately with Fritz Wehner. Some even had Luke pegged as a coward, noting that he had dropped out of previous flights claiming to have engine trouble and had seen very little combat. But the way he pressed the attack on the balloon over Marieulles was anything but cowardly.

Unfortunately, Luke's relationship with his squadron mates would have to worsen before it would improve.

The patrol crossed the battlelines just west of Verdun and continued east. As they passed over the hamlet of Abaucort, Luke spotted an enemy balloon tethered next to Boinville, a town situated along the River Orme. Luke broke formation and zoomed in for the attack.

Once again the enemy *Archie* batteries began sending up a barrage of flak and the winch crews worked frantically to reel the balloon into its protective pit. The balloon observer grabbed a light machine gun and began firing at the oncoming Spad.

Luke made his first pass with the left Vickers gun pouring out a steady stream of incendiary bullets. As he wheeled around for another run at the balloon, he saw the observer drop the machine gun and leap from the swaying gondola. Luke ignored the blossoming parachute and concentrated on the balloon, firing at the steadily sinking *Drachen* until the left gun jammed.

Luke banked away from the antiaircraft fire and managed to clear the stoppage before attacking again. In fact, he attacked *four* more times, having to clear yet another malfunction of his Vickers guns. On his final pass, Luke decided to give back a little of what he had received from the antiaircraft crews and strafed one of the batteries, the gunners darting away in several directions. The rapidly deflating balloon sank toward ground but somehow did not catch fire.

While Luke struck at the antiaircraft guns, Lieutenant Leo Dawson dove into the fray, his tracer bullets also lancing the canvas of the balloon. Dawson made two more attack runs before running out of ammunition. As the withering balloon draped across the French field, Lieutenant Thomas Lennon made a single pass, firing a 100-round burst. Miraculously, the balloon still did not explode.

All twelve Spads of the morning patrol returned safely to the Rembercourt aerodrome. The pilots inspected the damage done to their planes and once again, Luke's Spad was liberally pockmarked with bullet holes. The men reviewed the action to one another the way fighter pilots do the world over, tracing their hands through the air to simulate the movements of aircraft.

"Why didn't you get that observer?" somebody asked Luke.

Frank's answer was reminiscent of the episode involving the buzzard in the Superstition Mountains.

"Aw, hell," Luke replied. "The poor guy was helpless."

Any good-natured conversation came to an end when Luke, Dawson and Lennon all claimed credit for destroying the balloon. The three filed separate reports detailing their roles in the attack, and stated they last saw the balloon "on the ground in a very flabby condition."

Dawson and Lennon were of the opinion that Luke played the lesser role in the destruction of the balloon, for they were the ones that delivered the final blows. Luke disagreed, believing that he had obviously caused the most damage, having made six separate attacks. Captain Grant found himself playing the role of arbitrator in the dispute. The argument was settled, more or less, when it was decided that all three of them would be credited with a kill. At the time it was not Army policy to award partial credit for air-to-air victories.

That same day, reports began to arrive at the headquarters of I Corps of the U.S. First Army that a German observation balloon was aloft near the village of Buzy. The enemy was attempting to make a stand on I Corps' right flank, and the balloon was directing effective artillery fire that was stalling the advance.

The report was passed on to Billy Mitchell's air staff, who then telephoned Harold Hartney at First Pursuit Group headquarters. The directive was clear: the balloon over Buzy had to go. After Hartney issued the warning order to Grant, a delegation of officers from the 27th Squadron crossed the field to the Group operations shack.

There were four of them: Grant himself, First Lieutenant Kenneth Clapp (Luke's flight leader and therefore his immediate superior), along with the disgruntled Dawson and Lennon.

They wanted Luke out of the Eagle Squadron.

Luke was a "menace to morale," Clapp told Hartney. Then, in less than delicate terms, he put forth a proposal. Luke would be the shooter on the next mission, and if successful, he would stay in the 27th Squadron. If he failed, and survived, Hartney would transfer him to another unit.

Hartney could scarcely believe what he was hearing, but instead of reprimanding the insubordinate Grant and Clapp, he went along with the idea. If the cowboy scored, they would have to learn to live with Luke and quit complaining about him. If he failed, transferring him to another squadron would be easy enough.

Nine Spads were re-fueled and re-armed for the mission. It was decided that Luke and Wehner would accompany a patrol commanded by Jerry Vasconcelles and drop out of formation as they neared Buzy. Luke would be the shooter and Wehner would watch his back. It would be an arrangement the pair would use several times in the coming days with great success.

At 2:30 in the afternoon the flight departed Rembercourt, crossed high over the Meuse and the carnage of the trench lines near Verdun, then headed northeast for Buzy. Their target hung lazily in the crisp autumn air above the shell-shattered village, just downstream from Boinville where they had been that same morning.

Luke signaled to Wehner and the two Spads peeled off from the formation. Wehner climbed for height while Luke raced in at full throttle, the German gunners filling the air around the Spad with deadly *archie* bursts. The other members of the patrol gasped in disbelief as they watched Luke roar in closer and closer, as if he intended to ram the balloon. At what seemed like the last possible moment they saw puffs of gunsmoke trailing from the Spad and a stream of flaming .303 rounds stitching the fabric of the swollen sausage. Almost immediately it caught fire and began fluttering earthward, it's steel tether limp with slack.

Luke climbed away from the black bursts of antiaircraft fire. He had spotted another balloon hanging over the nearby town of Waroq, but had to repair the twin Vickers guns first. They had both jammed during his run at the *Drachen* over Buzy.

Suddenly the wood and taut fabric of the Spad was ripped with several crackling blows. From out of the sun came eight German Fokker D-7 fighters. Two of them were right on his tail, the muzzles of their machine guns flickering.

Again, Harold Hartney's training came into play. Luke broke into a hard turn to shake the enemy fighters, but the lead pair still followed. A hail of tracers smashed through the wings and fuselage of the Spad but the rugged craft continued to fly.

Luke looked back in time to see a stubby American fighter plane plunge straight through the gang of Fokker D-7s with its guns blazing. Startled, the two Germans on Luke's tail banked into steep evasive turns and vanished. Luke raced for the safety of the American lines, and was soon joined alongside by the pilot that had chased the enemy from his tail and saved his life.

It was Joe Wehner.

*   *   *   *

Back at First Pursuit Group Headquarters at Rembercourt, Hartney was listening to two of the same officers that wanted Luke kicked out of their squadron now offering emotional tributes to his skill and bravery. In the confusion that often accompanied aerial combat no one had seen Luke crash, but after torching the balloon over Buzy he had been jumped by eight Fokkers and was surely dead. Clapp had tried to come to Luke's aid and had succeeded in shooting down one of the enemy planes. Both he and Dawson rambled on about how unfairly Luke had been treated by his peers, and lamented his unfortunate loss.

"He's gone, poor kid, but he went down in a blaze of glory," said Clapp, choked with emotion.

The telephone rang. It was the operations officer of the 27th Squadron. Luke had not only returned from the dead, but wanted to trade his shot-up Spad for new one and go after the other balloon. Grant and Luke were going at it toe-to-toe and the Major had better hurry.

"He's crazy as a bed bug, that man," the operations officer said of Luke.

At the 27th Squadron hangars, the mechanics were once again shaking their heads in awe. Luke's Spad had been shot to ribbons and it was a wonder he had returned at all. The extent of the damage did not seem to make much of an impression on Luke, who was busy trying to talk another pilot into loaning him his plane. Luke wanted to fly yet another mission to get the balloon over Waroq.

When Captain Grant was advised of Luke's intentions he had immediately marched out to the hangars to confront him. Second Lieutenants do not write mission orders or change aircraft assignments, Grant informed him. When Luke protested, the row had intensified to the point that the squadron operations officer telephoned Major Hartney.

Hartney, Dawson and Clapp hurried to the Eagle Squadron's hangars, where they found Grant busily chewing-out Luke. When Luke made an anxious plea to Hartney to authorize the flight, Grant exploded.

"Who's running this outfit, major? You or I?" he demanded.

Grant was right, and Hartney knew it. Allowing Luke to circumvent the chain-of-command and obtain permission from Hartney would be seriously damaging to the unit discipline. Luke was crestfallen.

Joe Wehner went after the balloon without Luke, but as he arrived over Waroq, the *Drachen* was destroyed by French Ace-of-Aces Rene Fonck. Wehner tangled with a group of Fokker D-7s that were supposed to be protecting the German balloon line and shot down two of them before heading for home.

Chapter Seven

The next morning, Frank Luke was at it again. Over the next three days he would fly and fight like a man possessed. When 15 September 1918 was over, both Luke and Joe Wehner would earn the coveted title of "ace."

How Frank and Joe managed to find time to sleep during these incredibly busy days is unclear. The First Army was working hard to exploit the success of its offensive and the tempo of operations at Rembercourt steadily increased. When he wasn't flying, Luke kept busy in the repair sheds alongside the enlisted mechanics, wary of previous failures of both Hisso engines and Vickers guns. Luke not only oversaw but participated in the maintenance of his Spad, a trait that endeared him to the hard-working ground crews.

Luke took part in the dawn patrol of 15 September, which was uneventful. Just before noon, another flight of Spads left for the front lines. Grant had once again designated Luke and Wehner as the balloon hunter-killer team, but the troublesome Hisso of Wehner's Spad caused him to remain behind.

As the Spads winged northward over the rapidly-shrinking Saint Mihiel salient, Luke saw that the stubborn German balloon company at Boinville had yet another *Drachen* aloft. Luke left formation and sped in for the attack, sent 125 rounds of fiery tracer toward the balloon and watched it drift downward in flames.

Luke did not turn back to rejoin the members of his patrol, for he had spotted another target. High above Bois d'Hingry, a wooded area a few kilometers north of the River Orme hamlets of Buzy and Boinville, another kite balloon wallowed in the mist. The observer took to his parachute as the Spad charged in with its machine guns hammering. Luke scarcely had time to watch the balloon burn. From high above him came a flashing of reflected sunlight, the roar of engines and the rapid popping sound of gunfire.

This time there were seven airplanes after him, all with black crosses on their wingtips. As if to disprove those who believed he was suicidal, Luke sped toward the American lines as fast as the Spad could carry him, the gang of German fighters in hot pursuit. It had become obvious to the Germans that their American foes had a talented new balloon buster in their ranks, but they were about to exterminate this pest.

Suddenly a burst of .303 slugs ripped through one of the pursuing German planes, which spun violently and crashed into the French countryside. A lone Spad was racing in for a counterattack, firing at the Germans on Luke's tail. Together the two Americans raced southward, their speedy French Spads leaving the Germans behind.

Once again Luke's trusted friend had come to his rescue. Frank would later learn that Joe Wehner had solved the problem with his engine and took off to catch up with the patrol, destroying an enemy balloon near Verdun before he spotted Frank in trouble.

Back at Rembercourt, the weary maintenance crews went back to work on Luke's Spad. Mechanics serviced the Hisso and topped-off the fuel tanks, armorers cleaned the Vickers guns and fed new belts of ammunition into the breaches, airframe specialists repaired the damage done by a dozen bullet strikes.

That afternoon Joe Wehner departed on an offensive patrol to find another enemy balloon reported to be north of Verdun. Some accounts state that Luke also flew this mission without encountering the enemy, others state that his Spad was not yet ready and he had to remain behind.

At any rate, Wehner located the enemy balloon near Verdun and destroyed it. As he turned for home, he spotted an American two-seater observation plane in the distance, desperately trying to fight-off eight German Fokker D-7s. Joe raced over to help, scattering the enemy attackers and sending one down in flames. Joe then escorted the two-seater into friendly territory. For this action Wehner would later be awarded the Distinguished Service Cross.

* * * *

Throughout military history, the German soldier has been recognized for his efficiency and attention to detail. Sometimes, however, he is efficient to a fault. Reared in a highly regimented society and trained with unbending discipline, the German soldier is most comfortable when adhering to a strict routine. This mindset often led to predictable patterns of behavior throughout any given day. A sort of habitual timeclock-punching practiced by German fighter pilots in September of 1918 gave Frank Luke an idea.

During the Great War, flying a single-seat fighter plane at night was considered to be highly dangerous, especially in eastern France with its rolling hills, church steeples and wooded thickets. In the days before landing lights and luminous instrument panels, most pilots wanted to be on the ground before dark.

Observation balloons, on the other hand, often stayed aloft until just after sundown in order to get a final impression of enemy activity before bedding-down for the night. This last peek was used to formulate night orders for artillery units. Frank Luke noticed that these two factors combined to create a gap in the defense of German observation balloons.

Though Harold Hartney was no longer Luke's squadron commander, Frank often went directly to him with ideas and requests, a habit that irritated Alfred Grant to no end. One of these ideas was to attack the German balloon line just after the German fighter patrols retired for the evening and just before the balloons were winched down. The proposal would require Luke and Wehner to return in the darkness, but they felt it was worth the risk.

On 15 September, a day that had already seen Luke destroy two balloons
and Wehner two balloons and two planes, Hartney authorized Luke and Wehner to fly one final mission at dusk. As the shadows stretched across the battlefield, the two were off again.

Luke later reported that he saw several muzzle flashes from artillery on both sides of the lines as he crossed over Verdun. Luke spotted a light suspended in the sky at about 500 meters and flew over to investigate.

The light was coming from the gondola of a *Drachen*. Just as Frank had suspected, the balloon was still aloft hoping to get a final look in the twilight. Tracers poured skyward as the enemy gunners tried to stop the shadowy fighter, but Luke zoomed in at a low angle, his Vickers guns pounding. The balloon exploded in a shower of hydrogen-fed flame.

Luke turned south, hedge-hopping for Rembercourt. He was separated from Joe Wehner and soon realized he was lost altogether, spending almost two hours trying to pick out familiar landmarks in the darkness. Finally, Frank decided to put the Spad down and managed to land safely in a wheat field, then began hitchhiking back to the aerodrome.

It was after midnight when Luke arrived back at the squadron mess to find Wehner in the midst of a celebration. The two newly frocked aces congratulated one another and were toasted by the members of the Eagle Squadron. It had been an unbelievable day, to date the most successful in the unit's short history. It is doubtful that anyone still considered Wehner to be disloyal. As for Luke; he may have been hard to live with, but there could be no doubting his courage or skill as a warrior.

*   *   *   *

The next day the Saint Mihiel drive halted at a group of prepared German defensive positions known as the Hindenburg Line. The German air squadrons in the region were ordered to withdraw from their front line aerodromes and relocate around the city of Metz, several miles to the east.

On the morning of 16 September Luke and Wehner were once again prowling the enemy lines in the Verdun sector. Having learned their lesson the day before, the Germans had decided to take few chances with their precious remaining observation balloons. It seemed that observers were on the lookout for Spads as much as they were for artillery targets. Luke and Wehner spotted two enemy balloons that morning but the sausages were quickly hauled down before they could get near them.

Luke carefully noted the positions of the balloons, and that afternoon he approached Major Hartney with another request to sortie at dusk. Hartney agreed, and arranged to have lighting and signal rockets available to guide Luke and Wehner back to a safe landing. He also telephoned Colonel Billy Mitchell at First Army headquarters and invited the air commander to drive out to Rembercourt that evening at six o'clock "to watch the show."

As dusk began to settle, Colonel Mitchell and other members of his staff arrived by car and along with Hartney listened to Luke's plan. Frank and Joe would take-off at about 1845 and attack three balloons north of Verdun at ten-minute intervals. Mitchell, a controversial figure himself and one of the earliest proponents of close-support tactical aviation and strategic bombing, was skeptical that Luke and Wehner could pull it off.

Mitchell, Hartney and Grant climbed a makeshift wooden tower to get a better view. As Frank walked across the grassy field to his Spad, he passed a group of 94th Aero Squadron pilots, including Captain Eddie Rickenbacker, the current American ace-of-aces with seven victories. The balloons, Rickenbacker later recounted, could still be seen with the naked eye in the fading light.

"Keep your eye on those balloons," Luke told the group. Like Mitchell, Eddie was rooting for Luke but thought the plan seemed rather ambitious and very risky. By this time the pilots of the First Pursuit Group had stopped questioning Luke's ability and courage. His sanity, however, was another matter.

"Luke was an excitable, high-strung boy, and his impetuous courage was always getting him into trouble," Rickenbacker later recorded in his wartime memoirs. "He was extremely daring and perfectly blind and indifferent to the enormous risks he ran. His superior officers and his friends would plead with him to be more cautious, but he was deaf to their entreaties. He attacked like a whirlwind, with absolute coolness but with never a thought of his own safety. We all predicted that Frank Luke would be the greatest air-fighter in the world if he would only learn to save himself unwise risks."

"Most guys didn't want anything to do with attacking a balloon," Frank's nephew Don Luke said. "They would maybe make one pass at a balloon and if they didn't get it, they'd get out of there. To make multiple passes...that might make him seem overcommitted, if not crazy."

The two Spads lifted from the Rembercourt aerodrome, their motors pounding out a flat roar. In the distance, artillery began a rumbling barrage. This was a request from Hartney to the local battery commander, in the hope that the muzzle flashes of American howitzers would distract the enemy observers.

Luke and Wehner passed over the shell-wracked city of Verdun and flew north along the River Meuse. In the dying light the two spotted the sausage floating over the village of Reville and attacked it just after 7 p.m.

Luke and Wehner rapidly closed the distance, their machine guns firing. They both watched as the flaming carcass of the balloon collapsed and plunged downward to kill the unfortunate observer, who had just taken to his parachute.

The two Spads climbed away from the vengeful fusillade of ground fire. Luke and Wehner became separated in the dark and Luke headed west for another *Drachen*. When he arrived over the city of Romagne at the edge of the Argonne Forest, Luke saw that the winch crew was trying to recover the balloon before he could attack. Luke put the Spad into a steep dive and fired a burst from his machine guns that exploded the balloon almost on top of the winch.

Flying along the Meuse near Verdun, Wehner saw the fire from Luke's second kill and turned toward Romagne. As he hopped along at treetop level he came across a third balloon being winched down for the night, and fired a single burst from his twin Vickers. The sausage immediately caught fire and sank earthward.

"Antiaircraft very active," they would both state laconically in their combat reports.

Back at Rembercourt, the members of the First Pursuit Group broke into cheers as they watched three balloons burst into flames over thirty minutes' time. Even the dignified Mitchell, Hartney would later write, whooped loudly and broke into a victory dance.

Guided by prearranged signal lights, Luke and Wehner found their way back to Rembercourt and landed safely, despite the fact that both Spads were horribly shot-up.

Mitchell and Hartney inspected the damage, shook their heads with wonder at how the two young men managed to survive, and joined the crowd that had surrounded Luke and Wehner.

A tall, slender pilot detached himself from the group and extended a handshake to Frank Luke, offering heartfelt congratulations for a job well done. Eddie Rickenbacker had learned the value of good sportsmanship after many years on the professional racing circuit.

Frank Luke Junior was now the reigning American ace-of-aces.

* * * *

On 17 September 1918, the two-man team who had destroyed fifteen enemy aircraft in less than a week took a well-deserved break. A day of rest would keep the German balloon companies off-balance and allow the mechanics of the 27th Squadron to catch up on their work.

Luke seemed to be in a fine mood when he and his pal borrowed a squadron car and went souvenir hunting. Frank wanted to find German machine guns and they managed to locate two of them in a shell-damaged house near the front. They spent the afternoon in one of the hangars at Rembercourt, happily shooting the breeze while they stripped, cleaned and polished the weapons. When Luke and Wehner packed the guns into crates to ship home, someone asked why they wanted to go through the trouble.

"You can't tell," Luke said jokingly. "Maybe there'll be another revolution in Mexico and we'll need them in Arizona. Maybe I'll start one when I get back!"

Captain Alfred "Ack" Grant spent much of the day wondering what to do about Frank Luke. While Luke had turned into a worthy combat pilot, he remained a commander's nightmare on the ground. The events of the last week, and the attention that he had received, may have emboldened Luke. He continued to show a distinct lack of regard for authority, especially Grant's.

Luke had developed the habit of taking-off for patrols "a little behind the formation, hoping to catch-up with it at the lines," as his combat reports stated on more than one occasion. Luke wasn't fooling anyone. He wanted to be free of the restraint of formation flying to cruise off on his own. There was some speculation that Frank would actually pull the choke lever on the Spad's Hisso motor to make it run roughly, simulating engine trouble, so that he would have an excuse to drop out of formation. Once the problem had been "repaired" he would be free to fly his lone wolf patrol. Lately he had made a practice of stopping-in to visit the aerodrome of the Cigognes, or "Storks," a French fighter squadron based nearby for whom Luke had developed an affinity. These visits were usually done on the return leg of missions and always without Grant's permission.

Then there was the matter of Luke going around Grant and directly to Harney to seek authorization for his twilight balloon-busting shows.

Now the current ace-of-aces with Hartney (not to mention Mitchell) in his corner, Luke would be even more difficult to handle. Grant, however, seemed to arrive at a solution. In a memo dated the next day, he recommended that Luke be advanced to First Lieutenant, stating that "vacancy exists in the new squadrons now being organized."

If he couldn't kick Luke out of the Eagle Squadron, Grant would promote him out.

While 17 September 1918 gave Luke and Wehner a chance to rest and allowed Grant to deal with a disciplinary problem, it also gave the Germans an opportunity to prepare a deadly trap for the American balloon-busting team.

*   *   *   *

At 4 p.m. on 18 September 1918, Frank Luke and Joe Wehner took-off from Rembercourt and headed east toward St. Mihiel in search of enemy observation balloons. When they reached the new main battle line several kilometers east of the Meuse, Luke spotted a pair of observation balloons near the Three-Fingered Lake, a familiar pilot's landmark on the eastern edge of the former salient.

As usual, Frank was the shooter. He threaded the Spad through some high clouds while Wehner climbed to a height where he could keep watch for enemy patrols. Luke tipped the sturdy fighter into a dive and dropped out of the cloud cover, firing a steady burst into the first *Drachen*.

Tracers ripped across the fabric of the balloon, which shrank and spouted bright red flames. Luke pulled out of the dive, skimming just above the tree tops as the enemy gunners blazed away with all they had.

Off to the west, Luke could see a flight of German Fokker D-7s angling downward to intercept him. He would have just enough time to make a single attack run on the second balloon before making his escape.

The target grew larger and larger before the Spad's whirling propeller. A burst of Luke's tracer slashed through it, and then it too erupted and wallowed to earth.

Luke put the Spad into a climb, searching for Joe.

Joe was still high above and some distance away from the balloon line. He had spotted the Fokkers that were after Luke and had fired two red flares, but it is doubtful that Luke saw the warning signal while he was concentrating on his strafing run. Joe was rushing downward to help, as he had many times in the past.

As Luke climbed to join his pal the Fokkers caught up with him, at least two giving chase from behind. Frank climbed higher to gain the advantage and saw that Joe was also in trouble. Joe was busy trying to fight-off three German planes that had pounced on him from above. That meant that they were facing *two* groups of enemy planes. Luke was still too far away to help his friend, and two D-7s were closing in on his own tail.

Suddenly Joe's Spad burst into flames and began plummeting earthward.

Luke banked his plane into a tight climbing turn and roared head-on at the Germans that had been chasing him. Both Vickers guns hammered, and the lead Fokker D-7 fell away into a nosedive and smashed into the ground below.

Frank turned to face the next German, firing another accurate burst from his twin machine guns. The enemy plane shuddered, and then it too went into a steep dive and crashed.

Frank recovered from the dive, scanning the twilight sky. There were no other enemy planes nearby. There was no sign of Wehner. Luke studied the landscape below and saw that the fight had carried him over the city of St. Hilaire, so he turned west for the American lines. Maybe Joe was nursing his wounded Spad home. Maybe the burning plane didn't belong to Joe at all, it could have been from a different squadron, the pilot joining the fight after seeing the balloons explode.

As he neared Verdun, Luke saw white puffs of antiaircraft fire. It had to be an enemy plane on the allied side of the lines,

Frank realized. German *archie* was black, allied antiaircraft fire tended to be white. Luke headed that way to see for himself.

It was an enemy plane to be sure, a two-seater observation plane known as a Halberstadt. A short distance away Luke could see that a flight of Spads were stalking the enemy plane. They had stork emblems painted on their sides. It was a group of his French pals, the Cigognes.

The Storks seemed to be herding the enemy snooper further into allied territory, and its observer-gunner was probably busy watching them. Luke rapidly closed the gap, fired a burst of .303 slugs into the Halberstadt and watched it fall from the sky.

* * * *

A short while later, the telephone rang in First Pursuit Group headquarters at the Rembercourt aerodrome. Frank Luke was safe, the caller said. He had landed after dark near a gun battery.

They could put him up for the night, but someone from Rembercourt would have to come and get him in the morning.

A witness had reported seeing one of the Spads go down in flames near St. Hilaire. Since Wehner had not returned and Frank was known to be safe, Hartney knew that Wehner had been killed.

Hartney decided that he had better be the one to break the news to Frank.

Early the next morning, he asked the Group's YMCA representative, a Mrs. Welton, to accompany him while he performed the unpleasant duty. He also thought that Rickenbacker; steady, mature and wise, would be a good man to have along. Eddie readily agreed. The three of them climbed into Hartney's car and started out.

They found a stone-faced Frank sitting beside to his shot-up Spad, parked in the field beside the artillery unit. When Luke saw who was coming out to collect him, it confirmed what he already knew.

"Wehner isn't back yet, is he, major?" Luke said quietly.

Chapter Eight

The affect of Joe Wehner's death on Frank Luke was immediately apparent. Any attempt to console him was met with a stony silence. Any attempt to congratulate him on his recent success was met in much the same way. The victories of the previous day – two balloons and three airplanes – raised Luke's official tally to thirteen and greatly added to his lead in the race to become America's ace-of-aces. But he scarcely seemed to notice, so deep was his despair.

Even before their friendship had been tempered by the fires of combat, Frank had brushed aside the unfounded suspicion about Joe and became his trusted pal when no one else would. In return he had received the type of loyalty that would cause Joe, as Rickenbacker would later put it, to deliberately sacrifice himself.

Among Joe's personal affects they found a brass pocket compass. The lid was engraved with the inscription: *For Frank Luke "Balloon Buster" from J.W. Sept. 1918. 27th/1.* A gift intended for a buddy who had recently become the ace-of-aces.

That night, Rickenbacker's Hat-in-the-Ring Squadron hosted a dinner in Luke's honor. Elizabeth Brice, Tommy Gray, Bill Morressey and Lois Meredith, four American vaudeville entertainers, were at Rembercourt for a morale-boosting tour and provided the entertainment. It was a fine evening, complete with music, good food and wine. It was as fun as it could be, considering they were all very far from home and in the middle of a war.

Late in the evening, someone lifted his glass and said, "I think it is time to hear from Lieutenant Luke, the new ace-of-aces." The partiers responded with enthusiasm, and there were chants of "speech! speech!" A blushing Frank Luke was hoisted from his chair and made to stand atop the cluttered table. Reluctantly, he began to speak when the music and hollering finally quieted down.

"Fellas," Frank began, "I haven't done anything except what all of us came to do. We are all trying to get as many Huns as we can before they get us. I've been lucky. That's all there is to it."

Even more somberly, Frank added: "They got Joe Wehner. I'll make them pay for that. There is just one thing I want you all to know: *they'll never take me alive.*"

*   *   *   *

The next day Hartney approved a week's leave in Paris for Second Lieutenant Frank Luke Junior. When Luke protested, Hartney made it an order. Still very sullen, Luke left for Orly on his way to Paris.

On 21 September 1918 *The New York Times* printed the following headline:

11 GERMAN BALLOONS
HIS BAG IN 4 DAYS
Lieut. Luke Also Destroyed Three Airplanes in the Same Period
USES INCENDIARY BULLETS
On One of His Flights the American Downed Two foes on a Few Gallons Of Gasoline

Luke was soon back at First Pursuit Group headquarters.

"Aren't you back early?" Hartney asked him.

"Yes, sir."

"Why?" the major demanded.

The exotic and enchanting City of Lights, the vibrant rush of revelers along gas-lit cobblestone streets lined with flower-laden kiosks and cafes, the music, the wine, the beautiful women...none of it had appealed to Frank Luke.

"There wasn't anything to do," he replied.

Luke remained grim and silent, his eyes containing that vacant look that a future generation of warriors would term "the thousand-yard stare." As he mourned the loss of his dearest friend he may have blamed himself, re-fighting the fight over and over in his mind, examining dozens of *what ifs*, thinking about what he should have done differently for each.

We shall never know. What we do know was that Joe Wehner's death changed Frank for the short time that he himself had left on earth. A twenty-one year old had been trained and commissioned and given a speedy fighter plane to fly, and his resulting sense of invincibility seemed to have dissipated when Joe Wehner was killed.

Shortly after returning to the 27th Squadron, Frank received a telegram.

> WE ARE PROUD GOD BLESS YOU – MAMA

The cat was out of the bag, so to speak. Luke had mentioned, in a letter to Bill Elder, that he had told his mother that aviation was the safest branch of the service. On the night of Joe Wehner's death, he had said to Hartney, "My mother doesn't know I'm on the front yet."

On 25 September 1918, Frank penned a short explanation to Tillie Luke in Phoenix.

Dear Mother,

I have not written for some days now on account of being so busy, as no doubt you have already heard. This is only a line to let you know that I am O.K. Now, mother, remember that I have passed the dangerous stage of being a new hand at the game, so don't worry, for I now know how to take care of myself.

Love to all,

Frank.

While Luke was on his Paris furlough, the First Pursuit Group had established an advanced aerodrome near the front lines at

Verdun. The air service would share the field with the same naval gun battery where Luke had landed on the night of 18 September.

The navy had been using the field for the placement of a twelve-inch gun, of the same type used in battleship turrets. Mounted to a flatbed railroad car, the weapon was moved on a special spur line. It was capable of hurling a huge shell over fifty miles and playing havoc with the enemy's rear echelon.

Jerry Vasconcelles' "B" Flight of the 27th Aero Squadron was chosen to man the new aerodrome. The field would be used as an emergency strip, a re-fueling point, and an alert field from which sorties could be launched when enemy aircraft were spotted in the area.

There is some speculation that Vasconcelles may have felt slighted when Grant was chosen to command the 27th Squadron. Many thought that Vasconcelles, an experienced combat aviator and flight leader, was the obvious choice to replace Hartney when the major had been promoted to Group commander. Like Frank Luke, Vasconcelles thought of Grant as a parading martinet, resented his strict cadet-corps leadership style, and was only too happy to accept the Verdun assignment.

Like the agile football tailback that he was, Frank Luke dodged Grant and appealed directly to Hartney to be transferred from Clapp's "A" Flight to Vasconcelles' "B" Flight. The assignment would be for administrative purposes only, for Luke felt that he should be allowed to operate independently from the Verdun field. There he would be out of Grant's reach and closer to the German balloon line.

In the late afternoon of 26 September 1918, Luke departed Rembercourt to attack enemy balloons north of Verdun. With him was Second Lieutenant Ivan A. Roberts who, like Wehner, hailed from Massachusetts. Near Sivry, a village tucked into a bend of the

River Meuse, the Americans spotted a patrol of five Fokker D-7s and decided to attack.

Frank got behind one of the enemy planes and fired several bursts of machine gun fire into it. The Fokker went into a spin and disappeared, and Luke was suddenly busy fighting off two others.

Like most dogfights, the engagement forced the dueling planes closer and closer to the earth, and Luke found himself at only 100 meters by the time it was over. His fuel tank low and the Vickers guns plagued by stoppages, Luke turned for the allied lines. There was no sign of Ivan Roberts. Roberts did not return that night and was eventually listed as Missing in Action. He remains so to this day.

When Ivan Roberts failed to return, Luke was once again stunned by the loss of a flying partner. The remainder of Luke's combat patrols would be flown alone.

On this occasion Luke's plane came through the fight unscathed. When he climbed down from the Spad at Rembercourt he was approached by Kenneth Porter of the 147th Aero Squadron.

"What, no bullet holes?" Porter teased. "You must be slipping."

"Oh you'll see," Luke retorted. "I'm letting everyone take a crack at the balloon over Bethenville. If, by the day after tomorrow, you all fail, I'm going to go on over and bring it in."

On or about 27 September, rumors of Luke's transfer request reached Captain Grant. The Eagle Squadron commander was furious. Along with this tidbit of information, Grant also learned that Luke no longer intended to perform his regular patrol duty with the squadron, but to conduct lone-wolf missions without orders.

Grant lodged a vigorous complaint with Hartney, stating that Luke was no longer controllable. Hartney did his best to calm

Grant down, but admitted to himself that Luke may be playing the ace card, as it were, a little too readily. Both Grant and Hartney felt that they were losing their ability to control Frank Luke.

Their troubles, as it turned out, were only beginning.

Chapter Nine

The next day, 28 September 1918, Luke made his way to the Eagle Squadron's hangars and ordered the ground crew to get his plane ready for a mission. The crew dutifully topped off the Spad's fuel tanks and fed ammunition belts into the Vickers guns. Soon afterward -- and without permission -- Luke took-off from Rembercourt and headed northeast.

Allied fliers had been unable to destroy the stubborn Bethenville balloon despite a series of risky attacks. As he had promised Ken Porter, Luke set a course for the occupied French village at a height of 500 meters. Arriving over the balloon launch site he found the target still in its protective pit and swooped downward with his guns firing.

"After I pulled away it burst into flames," Luke wrote in his combat report. "As I could not find any others I returned to the airdrome."

Just *which* airdrome is a matter of speculation among historians. It is at this point, as much as any event in the Frank Luke story, that the line between legend and fact begins to blur. Some researchers believe that Luke, fearing the wrath of Grant, landed at the advanced base at Verdun and filed his report with Jerry Vasconcelles.

Hartney states that Luke returned to Rembercourt and flew another patrol with the squadron, during which he had engine trouble and landed near a French balloon company where he spent the night. However, the chapter of Hartney's memoir devoted to Luke contains several inconsistencies with regard to dates and times.

Still others claim that Luke destroyed the balloon at Bethenville and then flew to the Cigognes' aerodrome where he spent the night with his French pals before returning to

Rembercourt the next day. This is the generally agreed-upon version of events.

On 29 September, Captain Alfred A. Grant was lying in wait when Luke's Spad touched down on the grassy field at Rembercourt. Ace-of-aces or no, Luke had left the base without permission and was Absent Without Leave. He had also flown another unauthorized mission. Luke took his time in reporting to his commanding officer.

"Where the hell have you been?" Grant demanded.

"Over at Cigognes," Luke replied, placing the combat report on Grant's desk. "And I got you another balloon."

Grant was at the end of his rope. In clipped military tones he issued a stern reprimand, citing Luke's shortcomings as an Army officer and informing Luke that he was not the one in charge. No more unscheduled lone-wolf missions. He would perform squadron patrols and fall into line like everyone else.

Luke informed Grant that he had planned a balloon hunt for that evening and had the permission of Major Hartney.

We'll see about that, Grant replied. Luke was grounded until further notice. Dismissed.

Luke turned and left the squadron commander's office. A few minutes later, a Spad bearing the number 26 on its fuselage taxied away from the hangar. The steady ticking of the Hisso motor crescendoed into a roar, and the Spad raced down the bumpy turf and lifted-off, turning to the northeast.

Some brave soul informed Captain Grant that the departing Spad was being piloted by Frank Luke.

Grant turned to his adjutant.

"Get Vasconcelles on the phone. Tell him that Luke is on the way. On his arrival he is to be placed under arrest."

"Then what?" the adjutant asked.

"First, I'm going to recommend him for the Distinguished Service Cross," Grant replied. "Then, by God, I'm going to court-martial him!"

Grant stormed out of the 27th Squadron offices and hiked the five-hundred yards to First Pursuit Group headquarters, where he confronted Hartney.

"I can't handle him unless you back me up," Grant said, fuming. In any military organization it was critical to maintain a consistent chain-of-command. Luke was constantly circumventing the system and Hartney, Grant felt, was letting him get away with it. The popular commander, teacher, and organizer was committing a major military faux pax, and Grant knew it.

"Luke says he is going on a balloon strafe alone and claims you okayed it," Grant said to Hartney. "What about it?"

"Yes," Hartney replied, though Luke had not yet spoken to him. "Luke is going up to the Verdun field for a balloon strafe but I have issued absolute orders that his plane is not to stir off the ground until 5:56 p.m." The time of 5:56 was when the sun was predicted to set on 29 September.

After Grant left, Hartney decided he had better go up to Verdun himself, and went out to the hangar to borrow a plane for the journey.

We do know that despite whatever had transpired over the previous two days, Luke was present when Hartney arrived at the forward aerodrome at Verdun on the evening of 29 September. The Group commander noted that Luke's Spad was being wheeled into one of the sheds by the ground staff. Luke and Vasconcelles walked up to Hartney as he climbed from the cockpit of a borrowed Sopwith Camel.

"Major," Luke began, "there are three balloons north of here along the Meuse. I can get all three if you let me go now."

"Okay, Frank," Hartney answered, "but not until sundown at 5:56."

Hartney, Luke and Vasconcelles repaired to the dugout command post. The field was very close to the front and had been shelled several times. Personnel assigned there kept their steel helmets and gas masks at arm's length.

Luke paced nervously, and Hartney kept telling him to be patient and wait for the sun to go down. Vasconcelles sought to ease the tension by playing one of his favorite practical jokes. The navy 12-inch railway gun was busy shelling the enemy rear areas, and its muzzle was just over the top of Jerry's dugout. The report of the 12-incher was so explosive that a man had to stay under cover when it fired, unless he liked having his ears bleed.

It took a while for the sailors to load the huge shells and powder bags into the breach between shots, and Jerry had a good feel for the interval. Just when he thought the gun was about to fire, he poured coffee for his two guests. The next blast from the 12-incher sent the canteen cups flying and sent Vasconcelles into convulsive laughter.

Just before dusk Hartney decided he had better return to Rembercourt and ordered his Sopwith Camel removed from the aircraft shelter. The plane's Le Rhone rotary engine coughed and sputtered but would not start. Vasconcelles and Hartney began helping the mechanics troubleshoot the problem.

Suddenly another engine roared to life a short distance away. Luke was getting ready to leave on his self-styled mission. He was ordered to shut the engine down and wait until the prescribed time, and the blond youngster from Arizona cast a sheepish look in Hartney's direction. Hartney shook his fist at Luke, who laughed for the first time in many days. Shortly afterward, the problem with the Camel's motor was solved and a still-irritated Hartney took-off for Rembercourt.

When dusk finally settled, Luke took-off from the Verdun field, but instead of flying up the Meuse he made a sudden detour toward village of Souilly. Flying low over the headquarters of the American observation balloon unit there, he dropped a message:

WATCH THE THREE HUN BALLOONS ON THE MEUSE
LT. LUKE

As instructed, the Yank observers did watch the three enemy balloons, and within minutes they saw the first one erupt into a bright orange glow. It was the balloon they had noted on their map near Dun-Sur-Meuse. It was very late into twilight now, and the Spad was barely visible as it flattened from its dive and headed for the next target. Within minutes a second *Drachen* exploded, hanging lazily in the air before it fell, showering great scraps of burning canvas to the ground below. It had to be the balloon tethered above Briere Farm.

At twelve minutes after the hour, a third rush of flame appeared just above the horizon and slowly sank out of sight. The First Pursuit Group received a call from the observers at Souilly. Confirmed: Luke had destroyed all three German balloons on the Meuse above Verdun.

The Rembercourt aerodrome was alerted to Luke's impending return. But as the night wore on, there was no sign of him. Vasconcelles reported that Luke had not returned to the Verdun field either. Perhaps he was with the Cigognes. Maybe he had to land his shot-up, barely-flyable Spad in the wheat field at Agers again, or maybe he had landed near another artillery battery to spend the night. Most thought he would appear in the morning, after once again hitching a ride back to the airfield.

Correspondent Frederick Smith of *The Arizona Republican* was present at Rembercourt that night. Later he wrote in a dispatch: "There was still the forlorn hope he would come roaring out of the northern sky with some new record of hairbreadth escape."

But Frank Luke did not.

Chapter Ten

There is a curious event recorded for posterity in the Luke family bible.

After earning his wings at Rockwell Field in late January 1918, Frank Luke Junior returned to Phoenix for a short leave before shipping-out for France. One evening, Frank's mother Tillie asked him to plant some flower bulbs in the garden of their new home on Monroe Street. Frank was in a hurry to go attend a football game, but he took a few minutes to dig several small holes, insert the bulbs, and cover them with soil.

On the morning of 29 September 1918, Tillie Luke went out to her flower garden. Late September in Phoenix is about the time that the desert finally begins to recover from the long sun-baked summer days. She found that the bulbs that Frank had planted were starting to bloom.

The blooms were sprouting through the soil in the pattern of an airplane. Family members could make out the shape of wings, a fuselage, and a tail.

"Mother looked very sad and said she thought something was wrong with Frank," remembered Frank's younger brother Bill many years later.

*   *   *   *

Frank Luke Junior was officially listed as Missing in Action on 30 September 1918. His name did not appear on any prisoner of war rolls provided to neutral authorities by the Germans. No allied observers had seen him crash. The German air service did not provide any information through a dropped message, as was sometimes done out of a courtesy among aviators.

So what had happened to Frank Luke? The last earthly sign of him had been three drifting, burning observation balloons along the River Meuse.

On 10 October 1918, Eddie Rickenbacker shot down a Fokker D-7 over Doulon, France. It was his nineteenth victory, allowing him to regain the title of American ace-of-aces. He would go on to destroy seven more aircraft before the Armistice.

Captain Alfred Grant wrote to Frank Luke Senior in Phoenix, trying to relay what little knowledge he had about the fate of the younger Luke. Apparently the letter never reached him. On 16 October 1918, Grant wrote a second letter to the Luke family patriarch, enclosing Frank Junior's final pay voucher and expressing hope that Luke would be found.

On 3 November 1918, Captain Grant recommended Frank Luke Junior for the Congressional Medal of Honor, America's highest military award. Grant cited twelve separate examples of

Luke's "gallantry in action and for exceptionally meritorious service."

At 11:00 a.m. on 11 November 1918 – the eleventh hour of the eleventh day of the eleventh month – the Armistice officially ending the First World War went into affect. After four long years of strife, the German people had deposed their ruling monarch and sued for peace. The most horrific and brutal conflict the world had ever known, that saw the senseless slaughter of a generation of young men, was finally at an end. The guns along the battle lines of France were silent. The world was now "safe for democracy," and the "War to End All Wars" had been won. Or so it was thought. A wave of joy and celebration swept through the victorious allied nations.

Not everyone felt the same sense of relief. Grant soon received a reply to his letter of 16 October, and it was in the desperate tone of an agonized father:

ARIZONA CLUB
Phoenix, Arizona Nov. 12 1918

Captain Grant
27th Aerial Squadron
France

My dear Sir,
I have your letter of October 16th, also check enclosed for $184 for my son, Frank Luke Jr. service for September.
You state in your letter that you are still of the same belief concerning my son reported missing as written in a previous letter. We did not get any other letter from you.
I assure you it would be a great comfort to get a letter from you telling us something of our boy.

Sincerely yours,
Frank Luke
2200 West Monroe St.
Phoenix, Arizona

In late November, a message from the German government to the Paris office of the International Red Cross stated that Frank Luke Junior had been killed, but gave sparse details. The news was printed in the 29 November 1918 edition of *The New York Times*. The newspaper cited the source of the information as Miss Marie Repson of San Diego, California.

"Weep for him, yes," physician Henry Van Dyke wrote in a letter to Frank's parents, "but do not forget to be proud of him and rejoice in him."

On 3 January 1919, the fate of Frank Luke Junior was finally learned. After the close of hostilities, U.S. Army Graves Registration Office personnel were charged with the unpleasant task of locating the bodies of deceased Americans in territory formally occupied by German forces. In Murvaux, a tiny village off the River Meuse north of Verdun, local residents directed American troops to the grave of an American aviator that they had buried on 29 September 1918.

The French villagers described the American as young, with light hair, a medium height and of heavy stature. The subsequent investigation took into account Luke's last known whereabouts and final activities, which substantially corroborated with the account given by the citizens of Murvaux. Another piece of compelling evidence was an Elgin wristwatch found on the body, the same type worn by Luke. It was determined to be "almost certain that this officer was Second Lieutenant Frank Luke, Air Service, whose nearest relative is Frank Luke, 2200 Monroe Street, Phoenix, Arizona."

In what came to be known as the Murvaux Affidavit, seventeen Murvaux residents signed a statement detailing the events of 29 September 1918 as they witnessed them. The affidavit, combined with the investigations of the Graves Registration Office and the American Expeditionary Force general staff, emerged to tell the story of Frank Luke Junior's final flight.

* * * *

After leaving the advanced airfield at Verdun, Luke attacked and destroyed the balloon near Dun-sur-Meuse and immediately made for the second target floating over Brier Farm at tree top height, while being chased by a patrol of German planes. Luke managed to destroy the second balloon before turning toward Milly, where yet another balloon was aloft. The Spad roared through intense antiaircraft fire and set the third *Drachen* afire before turning to pass over Murvaux.

As he crossed over the tiny French village, Luke spotted a unit of German infantry in the main street. He nosed the Spad down for a strafing run, Vickers guns chattering. Caught in the open, six German soldiers were killed and six more were wounded.

There was a stretch of green field, gradually sloping downward toward a little creek, just west of the village. The Spad glided to a hard landing, the polished wooden propeller ticking to a stop. Luke climbed painfully from the cockpit of the bullet-shredded fighter. He had been hit.

The enemy would soon come for him, but he was too badly injured to try to run. Frank decided to head for the tall grass and trees down by the creek. He could hide there, and there was water to drink.

Frank could hear them coming. Their sergeants were shouting orders. He could hear them fanning out, crossing the field, the grass crashing beneath their heavy boots, surrounding him. They were calling out, telling him to surrender.

Frank unbuckled his holster and drew his Colt 1911. He made sure that there was a round in the chamber and that the safety was off.

They'll never take me alive.

As the German soldiers neared, Frank lifted the big .45 pistol and opened fire. A volley of rifle shots crackled in response.

Frank Luke Junior collapsed onto the grass.

Afterward

They knew who he was.

The villagers of Murvaux had seen him before. He was the brave one, the skilled one, the one who attacked the observation balloons. He had come all the way across an ocean to fight the hated *Boche*, and if the Americans had many more like him, all of France would soon be free.

Cortlae Delbart and Voliner Nicholas brought a wagon out to the field where the young man had fallen. They wanted to put straw in the bottom of the wagon upon which to lay the body, and to put a sheet over him, but the *Boche* would not allow it.

They knew who he was, too. He had been the scourge of the German Army for the last seventeen days. Six of their men lay dead in the village center by his hand.

The villagers watched a German officer kick the body of the young blond aviator.

"Get that out of my way as quickly as possible." he ordered.

*　*　*　*

At a public ceremony in Phoenix on 30 May 1919, Frank Luke Senior was presented with his son's Medal of Honor.

The Medal of Honor is the highest and most prestigious award the United States can bestow upon a soldier. In order to be deemed worthy of this honor, an act must be performed with "conspicuous gallantry and intrepidity at the risk of life, above and beyond the call of duty." The Medal of Honor is therefore often awarded posthumously.

Luke received the Medal of Honor for his actions on 29 September 1918, his final mission. In addition, Luke received the Distinguished Service Cross for the events of 12-18 September.

The Luke family decided not to have Frank Junior's body returned to the United States. Luke's remains were moved to the U.S. military cemetery in Romagne, and Frank Senior believed that it was most appropriate to leave him there, interned with his brothers-in-arms of 1918.

"He would have wanted it, I know that," Frank Senior said.

Frank Luke Senior continued a successful career in local politics, later serving on the Arizona Tax Commission. Like their father, many of the Luke children went on to be prominent members of the community and raised many children of their own. Frank's younger brother Bill became a successful businessman, and the Luke family name is still well known in Phoenix. There are over 100 descendants of Frank Senior and

Tillie Luke. The old Luke estate at 2200 West Monroe passed through a succession of owners and was eventually damaged by fire. Sadly, the property is now a used car lot.

There have been many tributes to Frank Luke over the years. In 1930, the Luke family raised private funds to commission a statue of Frank that now stands before the State Capitol. A small border town south of Frank's Ajo stomping ground is named Lukeville. There is an exhibit in his honor at the Aviation Hall of Fame in Dayton, Ohio.

Perhaps the tribute that Frank would be the most proud of is situated twenty miles west of downtown Phoenix. In June of 1941, Luke Army Air Field was established. Now Luke Air Force Base, it serves as the advanced fighter training base for the United States Air Force and is the largest fighter pilot training facility in the world. Several generations of "fighter jocks" have passed through Luke, including aviators of many allied nations. Ironically, one of the base's major undertakings during the Cold War was the training of German fighter pilots.

*　*　*　*

In a study of the life of Frank Luke Junior, one of the more compelling findings is the number of differing descriptions of him, and how they seem to contradict one another.

Don Luke offered his explanation. "He was a young guy who went over there to do a job," Frank's nephew said. "Obviously he believed in himself and had very little fear. What I can tell you about the family, his father and brothers, and I buried all of them: there were no braggarts. They were down-home, simple, hard-working people."

Luke has been described as quiet, unassuming and shy, yet arrogant, boastful and swaggering; foolhardy and reckless, yet cunning and skilled. Some thought he was a self-serving grandstander, yet there was little he wouldn't do for a friend. The same young man who said that he wouldn't return from the war also said: "they can't get me."

Perhaps the answer to the riddle is that Frank was all of these things. One must remember that he was but twenty-one years old when he died, still in search of himself, new to the challenges of adulthood and still seeking to establish the parameters of his adult character. For many young men this is difficult enough without having to travel to a foreign land and fight in a war.

Perhaps he countered an inherent shyness by being outspoken. He believed in his ability as a fighter pilot and went to great lengths to prove wrong those who doubted his ability.

He learned the values of loyalty, service and friendship from a loving family and devoted friends, most notably from a quiet boy who was thought to be a spy.

He was shaped by the harshness of the desert, the coaching of a patient leader, and the ultimate test of armed combat.

In the end he very selflessly laid down his life, as did many thousands who journeyed to France with him.

Appendix A

Medal of Honor
Citation

LUKE, FRANK, JR.

Rank and organization: Second Lieutenant, U.S. Army Air Service
27th Aero Squadron, 1st Pursuit Group, Air Service.
Place and date: Near Murvaux, France, 29 September 1918.
Entered service at: Phoenix, Ariz.
Born: 19 May 1897, Phoenix, Ariz.
G.O. No.: 59, W.D., 1919.

Citation: After having previously destroyed a number of enemy aircraft within 17 days he voluntarily started on a patrol after German observation balloons. Though pursued by 8 German planes which were protecting the enemy balloon line, he unhesitatingly attacked and shot down in flames 3 German balloons, being himself under heavy fire from ground batteries and the hostile planes. Severely wounded, he descended to within 50 meters of the ground, and flying at this low altitude near the town of Murvaux opened fire upon enemy troops, killing 6 and wounding as many more. Forced to make a landing and surrounded on all sides by the enemy, who called upon him to surrender, he drew his automatic pistol and defended himself gallantly until he fell dead from a wound in the chest.

Appendix B

Murvaux Affidavit

The undersigned, living in the town of Murvaux, Department of the Meuse, certify to have seen on the twenty- ninth day of September, 1918, toward evening, an American aviator, followed by an escadrille of Germans, in the direction of Liny, near Dun (Meuse), descend suddenly and vertically toward the earth, then straighten out close to the ground and fly in the direction of the Briere Farm, near Doulcon, where he found a captive balloon, which he burned. Following this he flew toward Milly (Meuse), where he found another balloon, which he also burned, in spite of an incessant fire directed against his machine. There he was apparently wounded by a shot fired from rapid-fire cannon. From there he came back over Murvaux, and with his machine gun killed six German soldiers and wounded many more.

Following this he landed and got out of his machine, undoubtedly to quench his thirst at a near-by stream. He had gone some fifty yards, when, seeing the Germans come toward him, he still had strength to draw his revolver to defend himself, and a moment after fell dead, following a serious wound received in the chest. Certify equally to having seen the German commandant of the village refuse to have straw placed in the cart carrying the dead aviator to the village cemetery. This same officer drove away some women bringing a sheet to serve as a shroud for the hero, and said, kicking the body: "Get that out of my way as quickly as possible." The next day the Germans took away the airplane, and the inhabitants also saw another American aviator fly very low over the town, apparently looking for the disappeared aviator.

Signatures of the following:

Perton	Leon Henry
Rene Colin	Cortlae Delbart
Auguste Cuny	Gabriel Didier
Henry Gustave	Camille Phillipe
Eugene Coline	Voliner Nicholas
Odile Patouche	Vallentine Garre
Richard Victor	Gustave Garre

The undersigned themselves placed the body of the aviator on the wagon and conducted it to the cemetery:
 Cortlae Delbart
 Voliner Nicholas

Seen for legalization of signatures placed above:
The Mayor,
AUGUSTE GARRE
Murvaux, Jan. 15,1919.
[Seal of Murvaux]

Appendix C

Confirmed Aerial Victories of
Second Lieutenant Frank Luke Jr.

12 September 1918	Balloon	Marieulles
14 September 1918	Balloon	Boinville
	Balloon	Buzy
15 September 1918	Balloon	Boinville
	Balloon	Bois d'Hingry
	Balloon	Chaumont
16 September 1918	Balloon	Reville
	Balloon	Romagne
18 September 1918	Balloon	Mars la Tour
	Balloon	Mars la Tour
	Fokker D-7	St. Hilaire
	Fokker D-7	St. Hilaire
	Halberstadt	Verdun
26 September 1918	Fokker D-7	Sivry
28 September 1918	Balloon	Bethenville
29 September 1918	Balloon	Dun Sur Meuse
	Balloon	Brier Farm
	Balloon	Milly

Author's Note: Some sources count the claim of 15 August 1918. Information obtained after the war indicates that the Fokker claimed on 26 September may not have crashed. The Murvaux Affidavit states Luke shot down two Fokkers on 29 September 1918, with which he has never been officially credited. Therefore, it could be interpreted that Luke had anywhere between 17 and 21 victories. In any case, he would be considered America's second-ranking ace of the First World War. The Luke family notes that of the German observation balloons destroyed during the Saint-Mihiel offensive, 80% of them were shot down by Frank Luke Jr.

Bibliography

Armstrong, B. *Frank Luke,* Tempe AZ: Arizona Historical Society Museum archives, 1988

Brown, Carol Osman, *A Grand Old House,* Phoenix AZ: *Phoenix Magazine,* April 1977

David, Gabrielle, *The Story of John Campbell Greenway and Ajo,* Ajo AZ: *The Ajo Copper News* 8 November 1995 edition.

DesHetler, John SSgt USAF, *History of the 1st Pursuit Group,* Langley AFB VA: 1st Fighter Wing History Office USAF, 2003.

Hall, Norman S., *The Balloon Buster,* London: Liberty Weekly Inc., 1928.

Hartney, Harold E. Lt. Col. USA, *Up and At 'Em,* Garden City, NY: Doubleday and Co. Inc. 1940

Hartney, Harold E. Lt. Col. USA, Excerpts from official report to the War Department, Phoenix AZ: *The Arizona Gazette* 5-6 May 1919 editions.

Hornung, Charlotte, *Arizona's Frank Luke,* Phoenix AZ: D&L Press Inc. 1976

Knox, John, *Aces Up! The Fact Story of American Aviators in the World War,* Phoenix AZ: *The Arizona Gazette Volume XLVIII,* 1928

Luke, Don; interview with the author, April 26, 2012.

Rickenbacker, Edward V. *Fighting the Flying Circus*, New York NY: Frederick A Stokes Co. 1919

Rickenbacker, Edward V. *Rickenbacker, an Autobiography*, Englewood Cliffs, NJ: Prentice Hall, 1967.

Roosevelt, Theodore Jr., *Frank Luke Jr., Arizona's Great Ace*, Phoenix AZ: *The Arizona Republican*, 21 August 1927 edition.

Smith, Frederick, *With the First American Army on the Argonne-Meuse Front*, Phoenix AZ: *The Arizona Republican*, 1 November 1918 edition.

Todd, Robert M. *Sopwith Camel Fighter Ace*, Falls Church VA: Ajay Enterprises, 1978

Unattributed, *Congressional Medal of Honor Awarded to Frank Luke*, Phoenix AZ: *The Arizona Republican*, 30 May 1919 edition.

Unattributed, *Frank Luke of Phoenix*, Phoenix AZ: *The Arizona Republican*, 28 June 1919 edition.

Whitehouse, Arch, *The Years of the Sky Kings*, New York NY: Doubleday and Company inc., 1964

About the Author

Keith Warren Lloyd resides in Arizona. He is a professional firefighter, a freelance writer, and a U.S. Navy veteran. He is author of the historical novel *Cape Hatteras*.

Made in the USA
San Bernardino, CA
09 July 2016